Harvard Business Review

ON

PRICING

THE HARVARD BUSINESS REVIEW PAPERBACK SERIES

The series is designed to bring today's managers and professionals the fundamental information they need to stay competitive in a fast-moving world. From the preeminent thinkers whose work has defined an entire field to the rising stars who will redefine the way we think about business, here are the leading minds and landmark ideas that have established the *Harvard Business Review* as required reading for ambitious businesspeople in organizations around the globe.

Other books in the series:

Harvard Business Review

ON

PRICING

A HARVARD BUSINESS REVIEW PAPERBACK

The *Harvard Business Review* articles in this collection are available as
individual reprints. Discounts apply to quantity purchases. For information and ordering, please contact Customer Service, Harvard Business
School Publishing, Boston, MA 02163. Telephone: (617) 783-7500 or
(800) 988-0886, 8 A.M. to 6 P.M. Eastern Time, Monday through Friday.
Fax: (617) 783-7555, 24 hours a day. E-mail: custserv@hbsp.harvard.edu.

Library of Congress Cataloging-in-Publication Data
Harvard business review on pricing.
         p.   cm. — (The Harvard business review paperback series)
    Includes index.
    ISBN-978-1-4221-4658-3
    1. Pricing. I. Harvard business review. II. Series.
HF5416.5.H375   2008
658.8´16—dc22   2008031408

Contents

Harvard Business Review

ON

PRICING

How Do You Know When the Price Is Right?

ROBERT J. DOLAN

Executive Summary

TOO OFTEN WHEN managers think about pricing, the first question they ask is, What should the price be? In fact, what they should be asking is, Have we addressed all the considerations that will determine the correct price? Robert J. Dolan describes two broad qualities of an effective pricing process and provides eight steps to enable managers to develop and use such a process.

To work effectively, pricing efforts must complement an overall marketing strategy by sending a message that is in sync with a company's desired product image. Such efforts must also be coordinated and holistic. Proper pricing requires input from a number of people, and lack of communication or cooperation between them can make overall pricing performance dismal.

The eight steps that expand upon these principles assess the factors affecting price. Companies need to assess their customers to discover how a product or service is valued. Variations in the way customers value the same product may be turned to a company's benefit through clever pricing. Dolan analyzes factors that influence price sensitivity and describes possible pricing structures. He reminds managers to consider competitors' reactions and advises them to monitor final rather than list prices in order to have a true sense of what's going on. Finally, he discusses the significance of the customer's emotional response and suggests a method of cost-benefit analysis. The pricing scorecard included at the end of the article will allow managers to evaluate how well their pricing practices meet these guidelines.

PRICING IS MANAGERS' BIGGEST marketing headache. It's where they feel the most pressure to perform and the least certain that they are doing a good job. The pressure is intensified because, for the most part, managers believe that they don't have control over price: It is dictated by the market. Moreover, pricing is often seen as a difficult area in which to set objectives and measure results. Ask managers to define the objective for the company's manufacturing function, and they will cite a concrete goal, such as output and cost. Ask for a measure of productivity, and they will refer to cycle times. But pricing is difficult to pin down. High unit sales and increased market share sound promising but they may in fact mean that a price is too low. And forgone profits do not appear on anyone's scorecard. Indeed, judging pricing quality from outcomes reported on financial statements is perilous business.

Yet getting closer to the "right" price can have a tremendous impact. Even slight improvements can yield significant results. For example, for a company with 8% profit margins, a 1% improvement in price realization—assuming a steady unit sales volume—would boost the company's margin dollars by 12.5%.[1] For that reason, even one step toward better pricing can be worth a lot.

To improve a company's pricing capability, managers should begin by focusing on the process, not on the outcome. The first question to ask is not, What should the price be? but rather, Have we addressed all the considerations that will determine the correct price? Pricing is not simply a matter of getting one key thing right. Proper pricing comes from carefully and consistently managing a myriad of issues.

Based on observation and participation in setting prices in a wide variety of situations, I have identified two broad qualities of any effective pricing process and a "to do" list for improving that process. Not every point will apply to every business, and some managers will need to supplement the checklist with other actions that pertain to their specific situation. But in general, by using these criteria as a guide, managers will begin to set prices that earn the company measurably greater returns, and they will gain control over the pricing function.

Strategy and Coordination

All successful pricing efforts share two qualities: The policy complements the company's overall marketing strategy, and the process is coordinated and holistic.

MARKETING STRATEGY

A company's pricing policy sends a message to the market—it gives customers an important sense of a company's philosophy. Consider Saturn Corporation (a wholly owned subsidiary of General Motors). The company wants to let consumers know that it is friendly and easy to do business with. Part of this concept is conveyed through initiatives such as inviting customers to the factory to see where the cars are made and sponsoring evenings at the dealership that combine a social event with training on car maintenance. But Saturn's pricing policy sends a strong message as well. Can a friendly, trusting relationship be established with customers if a salesperson uses all the negotiating ploys in the book to try to separate them from that last $100? Of course not. Saturn has a "no hassle, no haggle" policy (one price, no negotiations) which removes the possibility of adversarial discussions between dealer and potential customer. Customers have an easier time buying a car knowing that the next person in the door won't negotiate a better deal.

The pricing policy for Swatch watches illustrates the same point. The company's overall message is that a watch can be more than just functional; it can be fun as well—so much fun, in fact, that a customer ought to own several. The company's price, $40 for a basic model, has not changed in ten years. As Franco Bosisio, the head of the Swatch design lab, noted in William Taylor's interview "Message and Muscle: An Interview with Swatch Titan Nicholas Hayek" (HBR March–April 1993): "Price has become a mirror for the other attributes we try to communicate. . . . A Swatch is not just affordable, it's approachable. Buying a Swatch is an easy decision to make, an easy decision to live with. It's provocative, but it doesn't make you think too much."

For Saturn and Swatch, the pricing policy flows directly from the overall marketing strategy. This consistency, or even synergy, of price and the rest of the marketing mix is a critical requirement for success.

COORDINATION

There are typically many participants in the pricing process: Accounting provides cost estimates; marketing communicates the pricing strategy; sales provides specific customer input; production sets supply boundaries; and finance establishes the requirements for the entire company's monetary health. Input from diverse sources is necessary. However, problems arise when the philosophy of wide participation is carried over to the price-setting process without strong coordinating mechanisms. For example, if the marketing department sets list prices, the salespeople negotiate discounts in the field, the legal department adjusts prices if necessary to prevent violation of laws or contractual agreements, and the people filling orders negotiate price adjustments for delays in shipment, everybody's best intentions usually end up bringing about less than the best results. In fact, the company may actually lose money on some orders, and some specialty items positioned to earn high margins may end up returning margins in the commodity range.

Such was the case at a major truck manufacturer. Marketing set list prices that were essentially meaningless because so many other functions then adjusted those prices for their own purposes. While salespeople chased volume incentives by offering the largest discounts they were allowed, finance and accounting were charged with making sure the company covered its variable costs on each order. In this case, the problem was exacerbated by shortcomings in the accounting systems, but the fundamental cause of the company's pricing dilemma was that the decision-making process involved people with different pricing objectives and different data. There was no coordinated process in place to resolve these conflicting objectives effectively. The company is still working on a long-term solution to the dilemma, but for the short term it has dealt with the problem by creating a separate pricing organization staffed by a group of senior executives that collectively acts as "pricing czar." The group is responsible for gathering input from everyone and then setting a price.

When considering the coordination of the pricing process, managers should ask the following questions:

- What is our pricing objective?

- Do all the participants in the process understand the objective?

- Do they all have an incentive to work in pursuit of the objective?

Proper pricing requires input from a number of people, but if there is no mechanism in place for creating a unified whole from all the pieces, the overall pricing performance is likely to be dismal.

Eight Steps to Better Pricing

Fitting a pricing policy to a marketing strategy and considering the relevant information in a coordinated manner are broad goals. The following eight steps deal with the essentials of setting the right price and then monitoring that decision so that the benefits are sustainable.

1. ASSESS WHAT VALUE YOUR CUSTOMERS PLACE ON A PRODUCT OR SERVICE

Surveys show that for most companies, the dominant factor in pricing is product cost. Determine the cost, apply the desired markup, and that's the price. The process begins inside the company and flows out to the marketplace. To establish an effective pricing policy, however, that process must be reversed. Before any price is determined, pricing managers must think about how customers will value the product.

Consider how Glaxo introduced its Zantac ulcer medication to the U.S. market in 1983 to compete with SmithKline Beecham Corporation's Tagamet. Tagamet had been introduced in 1977 and by 1983 was the number one ulcer medication and the number one selling drug in the world. Zantac, however, offered superior product performance: It had an easier schedule of doses, it had fewer side effects, and it could be taken safely with many other drugs that were not compatible with Tagamet. Thus, its perceived value to the customer was very high. If Glaxo had allowed product cost to drive the price of Zantac, it might have introduced the medication at a lower price than Tagamet; it might have used a "follow the leader" pricing strategy. But Glaxo instead relied on Zantac's perceived value to the customer, initially pricing the drug at a 50% premium over Tagamet. Within four years, Zantac became the market leader.

Northern Telecom's pricing of its highly successful Norstar telephone system demonstrates the same principle. In 1988, as Northern's senior managers developed the company's strategy for competing with Pacific Rim suppliers, they realized that initially, the inherent superiority of their product didn't matter; resellers would value Norstar only at the market price then being charged by most of Northern's competitors. Therefore, rather than considering Norstar's cost and setting a price that might have been higher than competitors', Northern's managers decided to introduce the Norstar system at the prevailing market level and then look inward to determine how they could reduce costs in order to make money at that price.

Northern's managers knew that over time, they could convince consumers that their system was better than the competition's; in other words, they knew that Norstar's perceived value would increase as the system proved itself in the marketplace. Although the system entered the market at a price below what it was actually worth, eventually, as Northern's competitors began to fight the commodity battle and lower their prices, Northern was able to maintain its price level, secure a price premium, improve margins as its costs decreased, and increase its share of the market.

In Glaxo's case, a conventional "figure cost and take a markup" approach would have resulted in forgone profits; in Northern's case, the result would have been a noncompetitive price and no sales. By turning the process around and letting value as perceived by the customer be the driver, each company found a better initial price level and the foundation for its future growth.

There are several ways in which companies can assess what value customers perceive a product or service to have. Careful market research is one way; managers also should tap employees with direct customer contact, such as the sales force, for undiluted information from the outside.

2. LOOK FOR VARIATION IN THE WAY CUSTOMERS VALUE THE PRODUCT

By customizing prices, a company can earn much greater profits than it could expect with a single product/single price policy, yet many managers fail to recognize the benefits of customizing products and prices for different customer segments. A product will often have a much higher perceived value for an "ideal" customer than it will for an average prospect. If this is the case, a company would do well to separate the markets or segments and charge different prices accordingly. For example, consider how Polaroid Corporation introduced its SX-70 instant photography camera. Polaroid knew that some consumers—such as people in the photo-identification card business—would place a high value on receiving pictures immediately and on knowing whether or not the shots had come out properly. So the company segmented the market over time. Initially, to target those customers who "couldn't wait" for the new product, Polaroid offered the SX-70 to dealers at a price of $120 per camera; end-user customers paid more than $200 on average. Two years later, to capture the wider market, Polaroid offered the SX-70 line at prices that were less than half the introductory level.

The same principle applies in any business. Airlines, for example, attempt to treat business and pleasure travelers differently by offering cheaper fares with Saturday-night stay requirements to the latter. By developing products with slightly different specifications from the same platform, companies can customize pricing for segments that value the product differently.

Customizing price not only is common; in some cases, it is the key to a company's financial health. Consider the magazine industry: The cost per copy of a magazine when a customer buys a subscription is dramatically less than the cost of a single copy purchased at a newsstand. Software manufacturers employ similar tactics: When they introduce a new version of a popular product, they offer discounted upgrade prices to customers who already use the old version. The manufacturers know that the users' ability to continue using the old version of the product makes them value the new product less than someone without the product altogether.

Simple differences in taste affect value variation to some extent—for instance, some people simply like Big Bertha golf clubs more than others. But managers will be able to spot value variation and opportunities for price customization by answering the following questions:

- Do customers vary in their intensity of use? Heavy users generally value a product more than light users, especially in the durable-product arena—golf clubs, television sets, cameras, and the like. Heavy users also may be more interested in added features or complementary products; a company can use ancillary products as a mechanism for differential pricing.

- Do customers use the product differently? Some customers will use a product differently from other customers, with a consequent difference in perceived value. For example, consider the coated air bubbles produced by Sealed Air Corporation, a supplier of protective packaging. The company recognized that for some applications of the product, viable substitutes were available in the market. But for other applications, Sealed Air had an immense advantage; for instance, its product offered superior cushioning for heavy items with long shipping cycles. Recognizing the extent of the advantages in various applications and understanding the value differential in each setting was the key to Sealed Air's product line expansion and pricing decisions. The insight helped the company grow from $88 million in revenues in 1980 to more than $500 million 15 years later.

In many situations, companies find that a particular application for a product has a perceived value that is smoothly distributed around a mean. The mean for different applications, though, can be quite different. Take the case of a computer manufacturer offering similar workstations for two different applications: secretarial support and manufacturing design. (See the exhibit "Same Product, Different Value.") The mean value of the secretarial application is well above the company's costs—but also well below the value of the design application. In such a situation, customized pricing can be a great boost to profitability.

If markets are sufficiently large and show different means, a company should customize its prices. In some cases, customization can be accomplished without altering the product. This is possible if no information on the product can be exchanged and if the product cannot be resold between markets. For example, the computer won't be resold from the secretarial segment to the design segment. If information does flow between segments or if the product might be resold from one segment to another, product customization

---

Same Product, Different Value

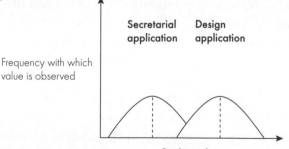

Product value

obviously would be necessary before prices could be customized. However, such an investment—in different brand names, software preloads, or added features—can well be worth it.

- Does product performance matter more to some customers, even if the application is the same? Before its acquisition by S.C. Johnson Wax Company, "Bugs" Burger Bug Killers guaranteed total pest elimination and commanded a price ten times the industry norm because it focused on those customers, such as hotels and hospitals, for whom the cost of failure was extreme. "Bugs" Burger's guarantee of "zero pests" had much more perceived value for those customers than it did for other potential accounts.

3. ASSESS CUSTOMERS' PRICE SENSITIVITY

Price elasticity, a key concept in economics, is defined as the percent change in quantity sold given a 1% change in price. If a company raises its price on a given product or service by 1%, how will the quantity of sales be affected? On average, the answer is that the quantity will drop by about 2%, but an "on average" answer is not very useful for managers trying to set price. Elasticities vary widely across product categories and even across brands within a category. Therefore, companies should analyze each individual situation. The most sophisticated pricing managers use market research procedures such as conjoint analysis to measure elasticities, but a good first step is simply to examine the important factors influencing price sensitivity in three broad areas: customer economics, customer search and usage, and the competitive situation.

First, consider customer economics. Price sensitivity increases—and a company's pricing latitude thus decreases—to the degree that:

- The end user bears the cost as opposed to a third party. For example, until recently pharmaceuticals manufacturers have had greater pricing latitude because neither the prescriber nor the patient paid the bulk of the charges.

- The cost of the item represents a substantial percentage of a customer's total expenditure.

- The buyer is not the end user, and sells his or her end product in a competitive market. Price pressure from further down a distribution channel ripples back up through the chain. For example, one steel producer was able to obtain good margins by selling a component to buyers who then produced specialty items for end users. Selling that same component to buyers who made products for commodity-like markets meant lower realized prices: The buyers were more price sensitive.

- Buyers are able to judge quality without using price as an indicator. In hard-to-judge categories, such as perfume, price sometimes has little impact because the consumer's assumption is that high price and high quality go together.

The customer's search for and use of a product affect sensitivity to the degree that:

- Consumers can easily shop around and assess the relative performance and price of alternatives. Advances in information technology have enabled consumers to increase their awareness of prices and access to alternative options. Over time, this ability is likely to lead to increasing price sensitivity for a wide range of products and services. Currently, sophisticated companies are using information technology to track supplier prices on a worldwide basis. Soon, consumers shopping at home by computer or interactive TV will be able to check the prices of many different suppliers.

- The consumer can take the time he or she needs to locate and assess alternatives. For example, in an emergency, speed of delivery may be crucial: Price will not be the primary factor determining the purchase.

- The product is one for which it is easy to make comparisons. For example, it is easier to compare cameras than it is to compare computers.

- Buyers can switch from one supplier to another without incurring additional costs. For example, Borland International, in marketing its Quattro spreadsheet package, stressed its compatibility with and similarity to Lotus 1-2-3 in order to position itself as an easy switch. This tactic put pressure on Lotus 1-2-3, increasing its price sensitivity.

Finally, regarding the competitive situation, a company's pricing latitude decreases to the degree that:

- There is limited difference between the performance of products in the category.

- A long-term relationship with the company and its reputation are not important, and the consumer's focus is on minimizing the cost of this particular transaction. (See the sidebar "Factors Affecting Price Sensitivity" at the end of this article.)

4. IDENTIFY AN OPTIMAL
PRICING STRUCTURE

Determining whether the company should price the individual components of a product or service, or some "bundle," is critical. Should an amusement park operator charge admission to the park, a fee for each ride, or both? Should an entertainment service like HBO charge by what it makes available or by how much viewers "consume"? Answering these questions incorrectly can be very costly. The resources allocated to thinking about pricing are often misallocated; most companies invest too little time, money, and effort in determining a pricing structure, and too much in determining the pricing at different levels within a given structure.

Two important issues to consider when creating a pricing structure are whether to offer quantity discounts and whether to offer bundle pricing.

Quantity discounts are frequently offered in industrial selling situations. For example, consider a manufacturer that must create a pricing policy given Buyer A and Buyer B, who value successive units of the product differently:

Units	Buyer A	Buyer B
1	$70	$70
2	$20	$50
3	$20	$40
4	$20	$35
5	$20	$30

For simplicity, let's assume that the seller knows these valuations and that one buyer will not resell the product to the other. The naïve pricing manager would say, What is the optimal price to charge? If the producer's cost is $20 per unit, the answer is $70. At this price, the company would sell one unit to each buyer for a total profit of $100.

The astute pricing manager, on the other hand, asks, What is the optimal pricing schedule? The insight lies in asking the right question. With the given cost and value parameters, the optimal pricing schedule will be as follows:

buy 1- $70

buy a second- $50 additional

buy a third- $40 additional

buy a fourth- $35 additional

buy a fifth- $30 additional

With this pricing schedule, buyer A would purchase one unit at $70, and buyer B would purchase five units— one at $70, one at $50, one at $40, one at $35, and one at $30, for total revenues of $295. Given the $20 cost to produce, the profits on those transactions would total $175—a 75% greater margin than that generated by the naïve pricing manager's optimal price of $70.

Bundle pricing is the second factor managers should consider when creating a pricing structure. For a manufacturer providing complementary products, like cameras and film, for example, the strategy should be to give up some of the initial profit potential on the hardware to increase the volume sold and consequently increase the potential demand for software.

Astute managers can gain a further advantage by also considering proper product configurations. The two products need not have a camera-and-film-type relationship to be bundled. Movie distributors often sell packages of films rather than selling individual film rights because the package values vary less across buyers than do the individual film values. Take the following two movies and their corresponding value to buyers:

	Buyer A	Buyer B
Movie 1	$9,000	$5,000
Movie 2	$1,000	$5,000
Total	$10,000	$10,000

Both Buyer A and Buyer B value the package of Movie 1 and Movie 2 identically at $10,000. If the company offers a bundle of Movie 1 and Movie 2, it can charge $10,000, yielding a total revenue of $20,000. If the movies are priced à la carte, on the other hand, the distributor would maximize revenue by selling Movie 1 to both buyers at $5,000, and Movie 2 only to buyer B for $5,000. Thus, optimal à la carte pricing nets only $15,000. Asking the question Should we price the bundle or the individual components? generates a 33.3% profit improvement.

5. CONSIDER COMPETITORS' REACTIONS

Pricing is more like chess than like checkers. A seemingly brilliant pricing move can turn into a foolish one when competitors have had their chance to respond. Price wars, for example, can easily be set off by poorly designed pricing actions. The lens through which pricing decisions are considered must be broad enough to permit consideration of second- and third-order effects.

Managers should ask themselves how any change in price will affect competitors. What will the competitor's first thoughts be upon seeing the change? They also should ask themselves, What would I do if I were the competition? And, Do I have an effective response to that action? Finally, they should consider the overall impact of the new price on the industry's profitability.

Consider how Eastman Kodak Company addressed its continuing share loss in the U.S. film market. In 1994, Kodak's share—70%—was still the largest among industry leaders, but it was declining. The company's flagship product, Kodak Gold, sold at a 17% premium over Fuji film. Kodak could have cut prices but that would have been a very expensive move. What's more, it is unlikely that such an action would have achieved the purpose of reducing the price premium over Fuji. With a 55% gross margin on film, Fuji would almost surely have matched any straight price cut to maintain relative prices in the industry. Kodak instead introduced a low-priced brand, Funtime film, in larger package sizes and limited quantities—priced lower than Fuji film on a per roll basis.

Most often, any pricing action a company takes will provoke some response by major competitors. American Airlines' shift to value pricing, for example, elicited nearly identical programs from Delta and United within days. Philip Morris's price cut on Marlboro cigarettes was matched by R. J. Reynolds. But competitors' reactions may not be limited to price moves; one company's price cut may provoke a response in advertising or in another element of the marketing mix. Therefore, posing the question If I cut my price 5% in this product market, what price action will my competitor undertake? is only the beginning. A 5% price cut could provoke a response in any number of areas. Southwest Airlines, for example, responded to American's value-pricing move not with a price move of its own but rather with an advertising campaign proclaiming, "We'd like to match their new fares, but we'd have to raise ours."

6. MONITOR PRICES REALIZED AT THE TRANSACTION LEVEL

The total set of pricing terms and conditions a company offers its various customers can be quite elaborate. They include discounts for early payment, rebates based on annual volume, rebates based on prices charged to others, and negotiated discounts. As M. V. Marn and R. L. Rosiello discuss in their article "Managing Price, Gaining Profits" (HBR September–October 1992), while a product has one list price, it may have a wide array of final prices. The real net revenue earned by a product can also be heavily influenced by factors such as returns, damage claims, and special considerations given to certain customers. Yet although it is this "real" price (invoice plus any other factors) that ends up paying the bills, most companies spend 90% of their pricing efforts setting list figures. Treating the real price so casually can cost a company substantial forgone profits, especially in an intensely competitive marketplace.

Price setters must analyze the full impact of the pricing program, measuring and assessing the bottom-line impact. The interaction of the various pricing terms and conditions must be managed as a whole.

7. ASSESS CUSTOMERS' EMOTIONAL RESPONSE

When managers analyze how customers respond to a product's price, they must consider the long-term effects of the customers' emotional reaction as well as the short-term, economic outcome. Every transaction influences how a consumer thinks about a company and talks to others about it. Intuit prices its financial software Quicken at $35, and some believe that unit sales would be materially unaffected in the short term by a moderate or even substantial price increase. However, Intuit holds to this price because the vast majority of consumers have come to view it as a "great deal." This perception has two valuable effects. One, it enhances Intuit's reputation with its customers, paving the way for the introduction and sale of future products. Two, the customers have become Intuit "apostles": They tell others about how good the company is and why they also should purchase the product. The pricing forgoes some profits now to create an important benefit down the road.

Of course, the same lesson cuts both ways. If customers believe that a company's product or service is unfairly priced (even if the price is, in fact, only slightly above cost), the negative message they send to other potential customers can be devastating for business. Some consumers have registered complaints with a company that offers database retrieval services, claiming that they were being "ripped off," even though the company was, in fact, saving them many hours in manual search time. The problem was communication: The company was not properly explaining how it justified its price. The solution was to increase awareness of the massive investment required in reformatting, indexing, and storing the data to make the service possible. Again, the key is understanding customers' perceptions. Simple market research procedures can be used to assess consumer reaction in terms of both perceived fairness and purchase intention.

8. ANALYZE WHETHER THE RETURNS ARE WORTH THE COST TO SERVE

An article by B. P. Shapiro, V. K. Rangan, R. T. Moriarty, and E. B. Ross ["Manage Customers for Profits (Not Just Sales)," HBR September–October 1987], introduced the notion of the "customer grid," wherein each customer is plotted at the intersection of the revenue he or she generates and the company's cost to serve that customer. In a world of logic, fairness, and perfect information, one might expect customers to line up along an equity axis with a high correlation between cost to serve and price paid. In reality, though, this expectation is seldom met; indeed, the authors provided an example in which there was no correlation at all. Although customer value is crucial in pricing, managers also must consider the cost side, being certain to avoid the infamous "strategic accounts" zone. (See the exhibit "The Dangerous 'Strategic Accounts.'") These accounts—and they are typically very large—demand product customization, just-in-time

The Dangerous "Strategic Accounts"

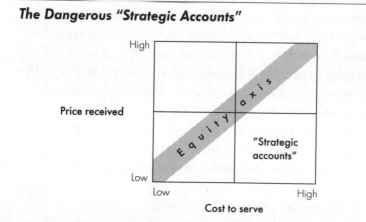

delivery, small order quantities, training for operators, and installation support while at the same time negotiating price very aggressively, paying late, and taking discounts that they have not earned. These accounts don't get what they pay for; they get a lot more. They are facetiously called strategic accounts because that's the justification given when account managers are confronted with the fact that the company is losing money on them.

High cost-to-serve accounts can be terrific—if the price they pay is high enough. One of the most profitable automobile insurance companies in the business specializes in high cost-to-serve customers (that is, people who have a high probability of being involved in an accident). While other insurance providers have shied away from these customers, this company has embraced them, but it also has made them pay rates commensurate with their costs and the fact that nobody else is willing to serve them. In terms of the map, this company was able to identify these accounts and push them well up into the top right. Big risk along with very big price can be a winning combination.

Similarly, a commodity parts distributor makes three times the industry average return on equity by focusing on accounts that order small quantities and have a proportionally high cost to serve. While competitors specify a minimum order of $400, this supplier accepts any size order—but its prices are 20% higher. Although this policy precludes getting the big buyers, the company is extremely successful. It has lots of small accounts situated firmly in the top right portion of the industry price/cost map.

Judging a company's pricing activities against the qualities and actions I have outlined will give a good indication of the quality of the company's pricing process. "The Pricing Audit" scorecard should help. Consider the two preliminary qualities and eight action steps outlined above. Add any elements you feel appropriate

---

The Pricing Audit

Our pricing process . . .	H-high M-medium L-low	Current performance poor　　　　excellent				
(Qualities)	Relevance	1	2	3	4	5
1. complements the overall marketing strategy						
2. is coordinated and holistic						
(Eight steps)						
1. assesses value customers place on our product						
2. considers variation in perceived product value						
3. assesses consumer price sensitivity						
4. identifies an optimal structure						
5. considers competitive reaction						
6. monitors the transaction level						
7. considers customers' emotional response						
8. analyzes revenue versus cost to serve						
(Your added elements)						

for your situation. Rate each item for its relevance, and rank current performance on the one through five scale.

An effective pricing process can't be created or implemented overnight. It is not a matter of making one or two sweeping changes in strategy or organization. Rather, it means getting lots of little things right and staying on top of the process to make sure that any improvements are sustainable.

Factors Affecting Price Sensitivity

Customer Economics

- Will the decision maker pay for the product him or herself?
- Does the cost of this item represent a substantial percentage of the total expenditure?
- Is the buyer the end user? If not, will the buyer be competing on price in the end user market?
- In this market, does a higher price signal higher quality?

Customer Search and Usage

- Is it costly for the buyer to shop around?
- Is the time of the purchase or the delivery significant to the buyer?
- Is the buyer able to compare the price and performance of alternatives?
- Is the buyer free to switch suppliers without incurring substantive costs?

Competition

- How is this offering different from competitors' offerings?
- Is the company's reputation a consideration? Are there other intangibles affecting the buyer's decision?

Notes

1. M. V. Marn and R. L. Rosiello report in "Managing Price, Gaining Profits," HBR September–October 1992, p. 85, that for the 2,463 companies in the Compustat aggregate, a 1% increase in price realization yields contribution improvement of 11.1% on average.

Originally published in September–October 1995
Reprint 95501

The author wishes to acknowledge with thanks the comments of Professors Earl Sasser and Ben Shapiro of the Harvard Business School and discussions with participants in the Advanced Management Program.

Pricing and the Psychology of Consumption

JOHN GOURVILLE AND DILIP SOMAN

Executive Summary

MOST EXECUTIVES KNOW how pricing influences the demand for a product, but few of them realize how it affects the consumption of a product. In fact, most companies don't even believe they can have an effect on whether customers use products they have already paid for. In this article, the authors argue that the relationship between pricing and consumption lies at the core of customer strategy. The extent to which a customer uses a product during a certain time period often determines whether he or she will buy the product again. So pricing tactics that encourage people to use the products they've paid for help companies build long-term relationships with customers.

The link between pricing and consumption is clear: People are more likely to consume a product when they are aware of its costs. But for many executives, the idea that they should draw consumers' attention to the price that was paid for a product or service is counterintuitive. Companies have long sought to mask the costs of their goods and services in order to boost sales. And rightly so—if a company fails to make the initial sale, it won't have to worry about consumption. So to promote sales, health club managers encourage members to get the payment out of the way early; HMOs encourage automatic payroll deductions; and cruise lines bundle small, specific costs into a single, all-inclusive fee. The problem is, by masking how much a buyer has spent on a given product, these pricing tactics decrease the likelihood that the buyer will actually use it. This article offers some new approaches to pricing—how and when to charge for goods and services—that may boost consumption.

Ask any executive how pricing policies influence the demand for a product or service, and you'll get a confident, well-reasoned reply. Ask that same executive how pricing policies affect consumption—the extent to which customers use products or services that they've paid for—and you'll get a muted response at best. We find that managers rarely, if ever, think about consumption when they set prices—and that can be a costly oversight.

Consider this example. Two friends, Mary and Bill, join the local health club and commit to one-year memberships. Bill decides on an annual payment plan—$600 at the time he signs up. Mary decides on a monthly payment plan—$50 a month. Who is more likely to work out on a regular basis? And who is more likely to renew the membership the following year?

Almost any theory of rational choice would say they are equally likely. After all, they're paying the same amount for the same benefits. But our research shows that Mary is much more likely to exercise at the club than her friend. Bill will feel the need to get his money's worth early in his membership, but that drive will lessen as the pain of his $600 payment fades into the past. Mary, on the other hand, will be steadily reminded of the cost of her membership because she makes payments every month. She will feel the need to get her money's worth throughout the year and will work out more regularly. Those regular workouts will lead to an extremely important result from the health club's point of view: Mary will be far more likely to renew her membership when the year is over.

For many executives, the idea that they should draw consumers' attention to the price that was paid for a product or service is counterintuitive. Companies have long sought to mask the costs of their goods and services in order to boost sales. And rightly so—if a company fails to make the initial sale, it won't have to worry about consumption. To promote sales, health club managers encourage members to get the payment out of the way early; HMOs encourage automatic payroll deductions; and cruise lines bundle small, specific costs into a single, all-inclusive fee.

However, executives may be discouraging consumption when they apply those pricing practices. People are more likely to consume a product when they are aware of its cost—when they feel "out of pocket." But common pricing practices such as advance sales, season tickets, and price bundling all serve to mask how much a buyer has spent on a given product, decreasing the likelihood that the buyer will actually use it. And a customer who doesn't use a product is unlikely to buy that product again. Executives who employ those pricing tactics without considering their impact on consumption may be trading off long-term customer retention for short-term increases in sales.

The Psychology of Consumption

Let's look more closely at why consumption is important and how pricing affects consumption.

HIGHER CONSUMPTION MEANS HIGHER SALES

One of the first steps in building long-term relationships with customers, we believe, is to get them to consume products they've already purchased. Research has repeatedly shown that the extent to which customers use paid-for products in, say, one year determines whether they will repeat the purchase the next year. One field study, for instance, found that health club members who worked out four times a week were much more likely to renew their memberships than those who worked out just once a week. According to another study, customers who regularly used an enhanced cable television service in one year were more likely to renew their subscriptions in the next year than those who used the service only occasionally.[1]

Consumption is important to the bottom line in many ways. In businesses that sell subscriptions or memberships—like Time Warner, the YMCA, or the Metropolitan Opera—customer retention is vital. But keeping customers is tough: Most magazines experience renewal rates of 60% or less, and health clubs retain just 50% of their members every year. As competitive pressures intensify and the cost of customer acquisition rises, a key to long-term profitability is making sure that customers actually use the products and services they buy.

Consumption also helps establish switching costs. In the software business, for example, companies often make more money selling upgrades than selling the initial application. Once customers start using an application, they have to either buy upgrades or make the painful transition to another system. Companies whose software is purchased but never used—shelfware, as it's disparagingly called—miss the opportunity to lock customers in for the long term.

Consumption is no less important for businesses that rely on a two-part revenue stream. For movie theaters, sports arenas, and concert halls, ticket sales are just one source of revenue; parking, food and drink, and souvenir sales are a profitable second source. *Team Marketing Report* estimated that the cost for a family of four to attend a major league baseball game in 2000 was $121.36. Only half of that sum was used to buy tickets; the other half was spent on beer, soda, hot dogs, programs, baseball caps, and the like. Clearly, if ticket holders don't attend events, these high-margin secondary sales are lost.

Still other organizations believe that their core mission includes encouraging certain kinds of consumption. HMOs, for instance, know that their clients' overall health will improve—and their own costs will be contained—if patients can be persuaded to get regular immunizations and periodic checkups. But they have limited success making this happen. By one estimate, 15% of insured children do not get all the immunizations they need, 30% of insured at-risk women fail to get mammograms within any two-year window, and 50% of insured men over 50 fail to have physical exams within any three-year period.

Finally, consumption is important to any business that relies on satisfaction to generate repeat sales and positive word-of-mouth. For products as diverse as wine, books, and PDAs, customers won't purchase again or evangelize about products if they don't use them in the first place. Indeed, it's difficult to think of any business in which consumption does not make a difference.

COSTS DRIVE CONSUMPTION

People are more likely to consume a product if they're aware of its cost. This is known as the sunk-cost effect: Consumers feel compelled to use products they've paid for to avoid feeling that they've wasted their money. It's well documented that consumers routinely consider sunk costs when deciding future courses of action. In one example made famous by Richard Thaler, a behavioral economist at the University of Chicago, a man joins a tennis club and pays a $300 membership fee for the year. After just two weeks of playing, he develops an acute case of tennis elbow. Despite being in pain, the man continues to play, saying: "I don't want to waste the $300."

In a similar vein, Hal Arkes, a psychologist at Ohio University, asked 61 college students to assume that, by mistake, they'd purchased tickets for a $50 and a $100 ski trip for the same weekend. The students were informed they'd have much more fun on the $50 trip. They were then told they had to choose between the two trips and let the other ticket go to waste. Amazingly, more than half the students reported that they would go on the less enjoyable $100 trip. For those students, the larger sunk cost mattered more than the greater enjoyment they'd get out of the less expensive trip.

PRICING DRIVES PERCEPTIONS OF COST

Our research also suggests that consumption is driven not so much by the actual cost of a paid-for product as by its perceived cost. This perception is influenced greatly by the manner in which the product is priced. Some pricing policies highlight the perceived cost of a paid-for product while other pricing policies mask the cost.

Consider something as simple as the method of payment. A $10 cash transaction feels different than a $100 cash transaction. Counting out currency and receiving change make a buyer very aware of the magnitude of a transaction. But a $10 credit card transaction is, in important ways, indistinguishable from one for $100— both involve merely signing a slip of paper.

Not surprisingly, people are better able to remember the cost of products if they pay with cash than if they pay with credit cards. In addition, they feel more pressure to consume products if they paid with cash than if they paid with a credit card. In one theater company we studied, the no-show rate for credit card customers was ten times higher than the no-show rate for cash customers. Other pricing tactics that mask rather than highlight prices—like season tickets, advance purchases, and subscriptions—also reduce the pressure to consume the product in order to get the money's worth.

Putting the Pieces Together

Because pricing has such a powerful effect on consumption, managers must make careful decisions about when and how to charge for goods and services.

TIMING

Companies often have great discretion about when to bill for goods and services. Some companies demand payment at or near the time the product is to be consumed—this is true when you buy a Big Mac or a movie ticket. Other businesses require payment far in advance of consumption. Concert promoters and sports teams have long operated on this principle. Health clubs and country clubs also charge large, up-front initiation fees. Finally, some businesses allow customers to pay long after a product is purchased. Increasingly, automakers and consumer electronics companies advertise "buy now, pay later" schemes.

Companies make these timing decisions based on either financial considerations (payment sooner is better than later) or demand considerations ("buy now, pay later" increases customer demand). But that may be shortsighted. Payments that occur at or near the time of consumption increase attention to a product's cost, boosting the likelihood of its consumption. By contrast, payments made either long before or after the actual purchase reduce attention to a product's cost and decrease the likelihood that it will be used.

We conducted a survey at the Chicago Science Museum in 1997 to determine how timing affects consumption. We presented the following hypothetical scenario to 80 visitors: "Six months ago, you saw an ad for a theater event and called to reserve a $50 ticket. Yesterday, you went to the box office and paid $50 in cash for your ticket, which is nonrefundable. This morning, you woke up with the flu. The event is tonight. Will you go to the theater or stay home?" Almost 60% of the people reported that they would go to the theater. They were not willing to let the $50 they had just paid for the ticket go to waste.

We then presented a slightly different scenario to another group of 80 visitors. This group was told that they had paid for the ticket six months prior to the event, rather than the day before. This time, less than 30% of the people surveyed told us that they would go to the theater. The only difference between the two scenarios was the timing of the payment. Yet that difference was sufficient to reduce the predicted consumption by 50%. The results of this as well as several similar surveys show that the immediacy of payment can be critical for the consumption of a paid-for product.

In fact, consumption closely tracks the timing of payments by customers. We analyzed data on the payment and attendance records of 200 members of a prestigious Colorado-based health club. All the members were contractually committed to one-year memberships that cost them $600 each. The club's pricing policies allowed members to choose from among four payment plans: annual, semiannual, quarterly, and monthly.

Members who made a single annual payment used the club most frequently in the months immediately following payment, reflecting a strong sunk-cost effect. But as time passed, the sunk-cost effect dissipated. By the final months, individuals seemed to be treating their memberships as if they were free and worked out at a rate that was only a quarter of what it had been in the first few months. The same pattern held for members who had paid on a semiannual or quarterly basis: Attendance was highest immediately following payment, only to decline steadily until the next payment. This resulted in a sawtooth pattern of usage, spiking in the first and seventh months for semiannual payment members and every three months for quarterly members. By contrast, the usage pattern of members who paid on a monthly basis was smoother. Since they were reminded of the cost of their memberships every month, they used the facility at a steady rate (see the exhibit "Consumption Follows the Timing of Payments). The timing of payments is important because it influences the club's retention of customers. Members who paid on a monthly

Consumption Follows the Timing of Payments

Our analysis of one health club's records showed that consumption closely follows the timing of payments. Whether members made annual, semiannual, or quarterly payments, club use was the highest in the months immediately following payment and declined steadily until the next payment. Members who paid on a monthly basis used the gym most consistently, making this pricing scheme the most likely to generate membership renewals.

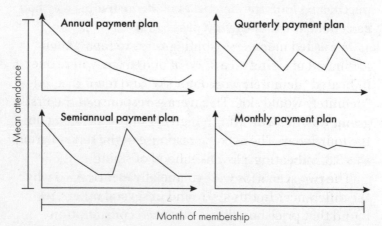

basis used the gym most consistently, making this pricing scheme the most likely to generate membership renewals.

PRICE BUNDLING

Organizations often bundle prices to increase the demand for products and services. This practice does increase short-term demand—but it may also reduce consumption.

Several studies demonstrate this tendency. We conducted a survey in a Colorado ski town, for example, presenting two slightly different scenarios to two groups of 50 skiers. The first group was told: "It's early spring in Colorado, and you're on a four-day ski vacation. The day you arrived, you purchased four one-day ski tickets for $40 each. It's now the morning of the last day. You've had three excellent days of skiing, but rain hit the area last night, making a mess of the slopes. A friend suggests that, rather than skiing, you take it easy and leave early to beat the traffic home." We presented the same scenario to the other group with one important difference. We told members of the second group that, instead of purchasing four one-day tickets for $40 apiece, they had each bought a four-day ski pass for $160.

We asked members of both groups to report their likelihood of skiing on a scale of one to ten, where one indicated "definitely would not ski" and ten indicated "definitely would ski." The average response of the first group was 7.0, indicating a high likelihood of skiing on the fourth day. The average response of the second group was 3.3, indicating a low likelihood of skiing.

The two scenarios were financially identical, so why the difference? In this study and in several others, we found that price bundling influenced consumption considerably. Quite simply, it is far easier to identify and account for the cost of an individual product in an unbundled transaction than within a bundled transaction. The one-to-one relationship between price and benefits in an unbundled transaction makes the cost of that item obvious, creating a strong sunk-cost effect and a high likelihood of consumption.

Nowhere is the impact of price bundling on consumption more obvious than in the case of season tickets. The purchaser pays one bundled sum for a collection of individual events, making it difficult to allocate costs to any one performance or game. This reduces the likelihood of its usage. We tested this out by analyzing ticket purchase and attendance data at a Shakespearean summer festival. The festival ran from June through August 1997 and involved the production of four plays. Some ticket holders had purchased tickets to a single play, some to two or three of the plays, and others to all four plays. What we found was that the no-show rate for people who had bought tickets to a single play was 0.6%, indicating that almost all ticket holders showed up. But the no-show rate for those purchasing tickets to two plays was 3.5%; for three plays, 13.1%; and for four plays, 21.5%. As the bundling of tickets increased from one to four plays, the likelihood of a person not showing up for one of the plays rose 35-fold.

One could argue that the higher no-show rate for those who had bought tickets to more than one play was due to other factors: boredom (ticket holders got sick of Shakespeare) or perhaps dissatisfaction (after the first play, ticket holders realized the quality of the performances was not very good). However, when we looked at only the first play each person had bought tickets for, the pattern remained the same. Compared with the no-show rate of 0.6% for the single-play ticket holders, the no-show rate at the first play for those patrons who had purchased tickets to two, three, and four plays was 2.8%, 7.8%, and 15.8%, respectively. So, the bundling of tickets had much the same effect as the advance selling of tickets in our earlier examples: It hid the cost of each ticket. Unable to link the costs and benefits of any given play, patrons who purchased tickets to multiple plays increasingly treated their tickets as if they were free. With little sunk-cost pressure, many of these customers did not use tickets they had previously paid for, reducing their likelihood of repeating their ticket purchases for the following season.

Linking Price and Consumption

We're not suggesting that executives throw out their current, demand-centered pricing policies and focus exclusively on encouraging consumption through pricing decisions. It wouldn't be realistic, and it wouldn't be smart. Many companies lack the ability (or the desire) to restructure their pricing practices. In some cases, industry norms or consumer expectations dictate the use of advance selling or price bundling. However, we believe that executives should take consumption into account when they set prices. Here are some suggestions on how to do that.

PRACTICE YIELD MANAGEMENT

Managers can run operations more efficiently by anticipating actual demand given the naturally occurring mix of bundled versus unbundled purchases or the ratio of advance to current purchases. Consider the case of a theater manager. She might forecast a no-show rate of 20% if the proportion of season ticket holders is high but a no-show rate of only 5% if the proportion of season ticket holders is low. Armed with this knowledge, she could better manage costs by staffing according to actual, as opposed to paid, demand. Alternatively, she could increase revenues by overselling some events and not others. In much the same way that an airline over-sells a flight in proportion to the expected rate of no-shows, a theater manager could oversell performances where the no-show rate is expected to be high.

STAGGER PAYMENTS TO SMOOTH CONSUMPTION

A second course of action, slightly more proactive but still within current pricing practices, would be to stagger billing cycles so that demand is smoothed over time. This is another form of yield management. Health clubs, for example, know that most of their new members sign up at specific times of the year, most commonly in January. But many still offer discounts to members who pay in full at the start of the calendar year. The net effect is that peak usage occurs in January, February, and March, which reduces customer satisfaction because of the strain it places on the facilities. Health clubs could stagger billing cycles to offset that trend. For instance, a health club could offer ten- or 14-month contracts, perhaps on a discounted basis, to break the cycle of January renewals. Over time, this change would help smooth demand and increase customer satisfaction.

TIME PAYMENTS TO MAXIMIZE CONSUMPTION

Some executives can do more than react to demand: They can use their pricing policies to actively encourage consumption. Perhaps the most dramatic way to do this is to link payments more closely to benefits. Consider Boston Red Sox season ticket holders, who are asked to pay for tickets five months before the season begins. To promote attendance over the course of the season, Red Sox executives could spread out that one large payment. They could, say, bill patrons in four installments. Customers might even prefer this approach because smaller installments are financially more manageable. Similarly, the health club we studied could increase usage and, thus customer retention, by promoting annual memberships with monthly, rather than annual, payments.

PSYCHOLOGICALLY LINK PAYMENTS TO BENEFITS

Some companies view price bundling as a necessary tool to promote initial sales: If they eliminate price bundling, they could eliminate the sale. However, organizations could psychologically unbundle those offerings to promote consumption. One way of doing this would be to highlight the prices of individual items in the bundle after the payment has been made. For instance, travel companies could itemize the approximate cost of offerings in vacation packages. Some all-inclusive cruise ships already make guests pay for drinks, meals, and entertainment with beads to highlight the fact that nothing is really free. Restaurants could offer the same dishes both à la carte and as part of a fixed-price dinner, so that the cost of each item in the latter becomes clear. In the same way, HMOs could promote preventive care by itemizing the cost of individual services within the bundled fee, making the cost of those services more apparent to the customer. This would increase enrollees' likelihood of consuming the benefits (getting checkups, immunizations, and so on) they've already paid for.

REDUCE CONSUMPTION

Not all organizations want to encourage consumption all the time. Consider the manager of a truly scarce resource, such as a private golf course on a beautiful Sunday morning in June. Managing peak demand is the main concern. The current alternatives are to limit the number of customers admitted, as when a country club caps membership, or to accept all customers and run the risk of dissatisfaction when the facility is at capacity. The first solution limits revenues; the second increases customer frustration. By managing when and how payments are made, executives can maximize the total number of customers who pay for their services and, at the same time, limit peak demand. If the golf course manager charges annual membership fees in January or February, long before the golf season has begun, a member's pain of payment will fade by the time the peak summer months come, reducing the need to get his money's worth. That should allow the club to maximize its membership base without turning away members wanting to play during the peak period. By contrast, if the club bills its members just prior to the peak season, say in May or June, it will be inadvertently promoting demand at its busiest time. Similarly, when vacationers at a ski resort buy a week's worth of lift tickets, the resort has the option of providing them with seven daily tickets or a bundled pass. The former will encourage consumption every day ("I'm not going to let today's ticket go to waste!"), while the latter will mask the cost of skiing on any given day and reduce crowds on the slopes.

M ANAGERS SPEND a lot of time thinking about how to get customers to buy their products and services. But that's just half the battle. If organizations wish to build long-term relationships with customers, they must make sure their customers actually use their products. A first step is pricing.

Notes

1. Stefano DellaVigna and Ulrike Malmendier, "Self-Control in the Market: Evidence from the Health Club Industry," Working Paper (Harvard University, 2001). Katherine N. Lemon, Tiffany Barnett White, and Russell S. Winer, "Dynamic Customer Relationship Management: Incorporating Future Considerations into the Service Retention Decision," *Journal of Marketing*, January 2002.

Originally published in September 2002
Reprinted R0209G

Managing Price, Gaining Profit

MICHAEL V. MARN AND
ROBERT L. ROSIELLO

Executive Summary

THE FASTEST AND MOST effective way for a company to realize maximum profit is to get its pricing right. The right price can boost profit faster than increasing volume will; the wrong price can shrink it just as quickly.

Yet many otherwise tough-minded managers miss out on significant profits because they shy away from pricing decisions for fear that they will alienate their customers. Worse, if management isn't controlling its pricing policies, there's a good chance that the company's clients are manipulating them to their own advantage.

McKinsey & Company's Michael Marn and Robert Rosiello show managers how to gain control of the pricing puzzle and capture untapped profit potential by using two basic concepts: the pocket price waterfall and the pocket price band.

The pocket price waterfall reveals how price erodes between a company's invoice figure and the actual amount paid by the customer—the transaction price. It tracks the volume purchase discounts, early payment bonuses, and frequent customer incentives that squeeze a company's profits.

The pocket price band plots the range of pocket prices over which any given unit volume of a single product sells. Wide price bands are commonplace: some manufacturers' transaction prices for a given product range 60%; one fastener supplier's price band ranged up to 500%.

Managers who study their pocket price waterfalls and bands can identify unnecessary discounting at the transaction level, low-performance accounts, and misplaced marketing efforts. The problems, once identified, are typically easy and inexpensive to remedy.

THE FASTEST AND MOST effective way for a company to realize its maximum profit is to get its pricing right. The right price can boost profit faster than increasing volume will; the wrong price can shrink it just as quickly. Yet many otherwise tough-minded managers shy away from initiatives to improve price for fear that they will alienate or lose customers. The result of *not* managing price performance, however, is far more damaging. Getting the price right is one of the most fundamental and important management functions; it should be one of a manager's first responsibilities, a nuts and bolts kind of job that determines the dollar and cents performance of the company.

The leverage and payoff of improved pricing are high. Compare, for example, the profit implications of a 1% increase in volume and a 1% increase in price. For a company with average economics, improving unit volume by 1% yields a 3.3% increase in operating profit, assuming no decrease in price. But, as Exhibit 1 shows, a 1% improvement in price, assuming no loss of volume, increases operating profit by 11.1%. Improvements in price typically have three to four times the effect on profitability as proportionate increases in volume.

With such extreme profit leverage, pricing is one function that a company can always improve. One consumer durable products company increased operating profit dollars by nearly 30% with a mere 2.5% improvement in average prices. An industrial equipment manufacturer boosted operating profits by 35% by carefully managing price levels up a modest 3%. According to our research, a wide variety of businesses, including those in consumer packaged goods, energy, and banking and financial services, have achieved comparable results.

Even if a company's managers make the right pricing decisions 90% of the time, it's worthwhile to try for 92%—the payoff is that high. But the price lever is a double-edged sword. The messages of Exhibit 1 also apply in reverse: a mere 1% price decrease for an average company, for instance, would destroy 11.1% of the company's operating profit dollars.

Pricing issues are seldom simple and isolated; usually they are diverse, intricate, and linked to many aspects of a business. But while most managers have a handle on the bulk of pricing issues, many overlook a key aspect of this most basic management discipline: transaction price management. Without realizing it, many managers are leaving significant amounts of money—potential profit—on the table at the transaction level, the point where the product meets the consumer. Most companies use invoice price as a reporting measure, but the differences between invoice and actual transaction price can mean significant reductions to bottom-line profit.

Some companies that have identified this problem are handling it by applying two basic concepts: the pocket price waterfall and the pocket price band. Reduced to their essentials, these concepts show companies where their products' prices erode between invoice price and actual transaction price, and they help companies capture untapped opportunities at that level.

The Three Levels of Price Management

The pricing puzzle is more manageable when taken in pieces. Price management issues, opportunities, and threats fall into three distinct but closely related levels.

1. INDUSTRY SUPPLY AND DEMAND

At this highest level of price management, the basic laws of economics come into play. Changes in supply (plant closings, new competitors), demand (demographic shifts, emerging substitute products), and costs (new technologies) have very real effects on industry price levels.

Managers examining pricing in this context should understand the pricing "tone" of their markets—that is, the overall direction of price pressure (up or down) and the critical marketplace variables fueling that pressure. This knowledge allows managers not only to predict and exploit broad price trends but also to foresee the likely impact of their actions on industry price levels.

2. PRODUCT MARKET STRATEGY

The central issue here is how customers perceive the benefits of products and related services across available suppliers. If a product delivers more benefit to customers, then the company can usually charge a higher price versus its competition. The trick is to understand just what factors of the product and service package customers perceive as important, how a company and its competitors stack up against those factors, and how much customers are willing to pay for superiority in those factors.

Market research tools, like conjoint analysis and focus groups, can help managers understand customer perception of benefits. And understanding at this second level of price management helps guide both the product's price positioning and the fine-tuning of product and service offerings.

Exhibit 1. *Comparison of Profits Levers**

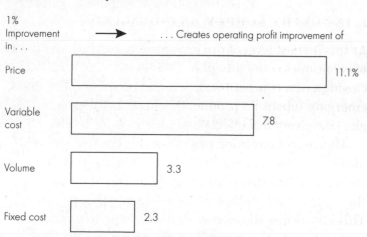

1% Improvement in . . .	. . . Creates operating profit improvement of
Price	11.1%
Variable cost	7.8
Volume	3.3
Fixed cost	2.3

*Based on average economics of 2,463 companies in Compustat aggregate.

3. TRANSACTIONS

At this last level of price management, the critical issue is how to manage the exact price charged for *each* transaction—that is, what base price to use, and what terms, discounts, allowances, rebates, incentives, and bonuses to apply. Where concern at other price management levels is directed more toward the broad, strategic positioning of products in the marketplace, focus at the transaction level of price management is microscopic—customer by customer, transaction by transaction, deal by deal.

The three discrete levels of price management are clearly related. If, for example, a company foresees an industrywide supply shortage of its product, repositioning the product by lowering the price would be a mistake. In the same way, the product's market strategy should set the context for transaction-level pricing decisions: a move by Toyota to discount its Lexus luxury sedan at the transaction level would conflict with the market positioning of that model as a high-benefit, fair-priced alternative to competitors like Mercedes Benz, BMW, or Jaguar.

Unfortunately, many top managers perceive transaction pricing decisions as unimportant and often relegate them to low-ranking managers or even entry-level clerks, with some flexibility at the sales force level. By doing so, companies may be foregoing one of the most substantial profit opportunities available.

The Transaction Pricing Opportunity

The objective of transaction price management is to achieve the best net realized price for each order or transaction. Transaction pricing is a game of inches where tens, hundreds, or even thousands of customer- and order-specific pricing decisions daily comprise success or failure—where companies capture or lose percentage points of margin one transaction at a time. But top management neglect, high transaction volume and complexity, and management reporting shortfalls all contribute to missed transaction pricing opportunities.

The complexity and volume of transactions tend to create a smoke screen that makes it nearly impossible for even the rare senior managers who show an interest to understand what is actually happening at the transaction level. Management information systems most often do not report on transaction price performance, or report only average prices and thus shed no real light on pricing opportunities lost transaction by transaction.

The pocket price waterfall and the pocket price band have proven valuable in lifting this smoke screen and providing a foundation to capture opportunity at the transaction level.

THE POCKET PRICE WATERFALL

Many companies fail to manage the full range of components that contribute to the final transaction price. Exhibit 2 shows the price components for a typical sale by a manufacturer of linoleum flooring to a retailer. The starting point is the dealer list price from which an order-size discount (based on the dollar volume of that order) and a "competitive discount" (a discretionary discount negotiated before the order is taken) are subtracted to get to invoice price. For companies that monitor price performance, invoice price is the measure most commonly used.

But in most businesses, particularly those selling through trade intermediaries, invoice price does not

Exhibit 2. In the Pocket Price Waterfall, Each Element Represents a Revenue Leak

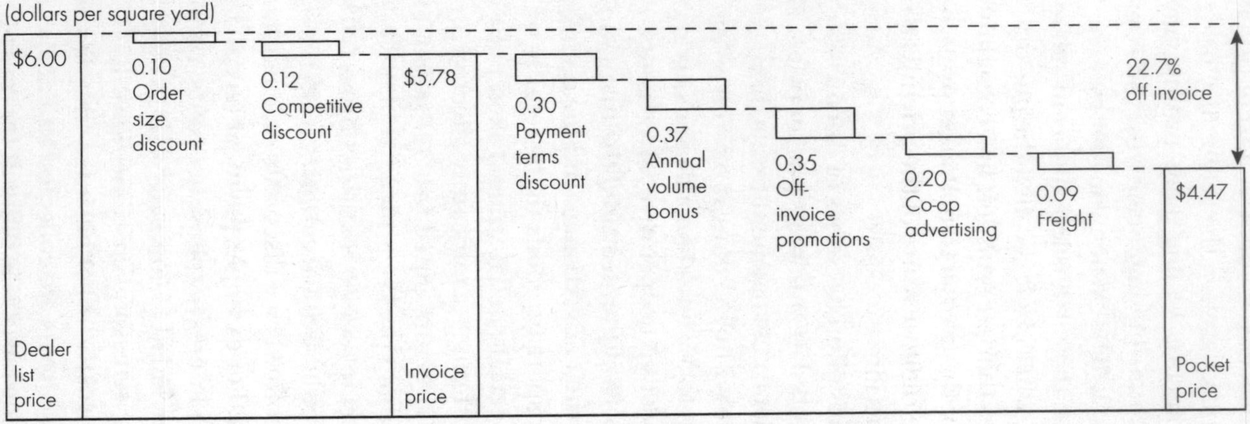

(dollars per square yard)

| $6.00 | | 0.10 | 0.12 | $5.78 | 0.30 | 0.37 | 0.35 | 0.20 | 0.09 | 22.7% off invoice | $4.47 |

Dealer list price — Order size discount — Competitive discount — Invoice price — Payment terms discount — Annual volume bonus — Off-invoice promotions — Co-op advertising — Freight — Pocket price reflect the true transaction amount. A host of pricing factors come into play between the set invoice price and the final transaction cost. Among them: prompt payment discounts, volume buying incentives, and cooperative advertising allowances. When you subtract the income lost through these transaction-specific elements from invoice price, what is left is called the pocket price—the revenues that are truly left in a company's pocket as a result of the transaction. Pocket price, not invoice price, is the right measure of the pricing attractiveness of a transaction.

The manufacturer offered a series of discounts and incentives that affected its product's pocket price. The company gave dealers a 2% payment terms discount if they paid an invoice within 30 days. It offered an annual volume bonus of up to 5% based on a dealer's total purchases. Retailers received cooperative advertising allowances of up to 4% if they featured the manufacturer's products in their advertising. And the company paid freight for transporting goods to the retailer on all orders exceeding a certain dollar value. Taken individually, none of these offerings significantly affected profit. Together, however, they amounted to a 22.7% difference between the invoice and pocket prices.

Otherwise competent senior managers often fail to focus on pocket price because accounting systems do not collect many of the off-invoice discounts on a customer or transaction basis. For example, payment terms discounts get buried in interest expense accounts, cooperative advertising is included in companywide promotions and advertising line items, and customer-specific freight gets lumped in with all the other business transportation expenses. Since these items are collected and accounted for on a companywide basis, it is difficult for most managers to think about them—let alone tally them—on a customer-by-customer or transaction-by-transaction basis.

Exhibit 2, which shows revenues cascading down from list price to invoice price to pocket price, is called the pocket price waterfall. Each element of price structure represents a revenue "leak." The 22.7% drop from invoice price down to pocket price is not at all uncommon. The average decline from invoice down to pocket price was 16.7% for one consumer packaged goods company, 17.7% for a commodity chemical company, 18.6% for a computer company, 20.3% for a footwear company, 21.9% for an automobile manufacturer, and 28.9% for one lighting products supplier.

Companies that do not actively manage the entire pocket price waterfall, with its multiple and highly variable revenue leaks, miss all kinds of opportunities to enhance price performance.

THE POCKET PRICE BAND

At any given point in time, no item sells at exactly the same pocket price to all customers. Rather, items sell over a range of prices. This range, given a set unit volume of a specific product, is called the pocket price band.[1,2] Exhibit 3 shows the flooring manufacturer's pocket price band on a dollars per yard basis for a single product. Note that there is a 35% difference between the highest and lowest priced transactions. Although the width of this pocket price band may appear large, price bands that are much wider are commonplace. Pocket price bands that we examined ranged up to 60% for a lighting fixtures manufacturer, 70% for a computer peripherals supplier, 200% for a specialty chemicals company, and 500% for a fastener supplier.

Exhibit 3. The Elements of a Pocket Price Band Reveal Profit Opportunities

(Percent of volume)

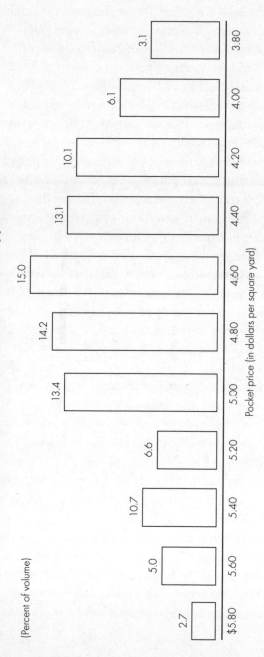

Pocket price (in dollars per square yard)

Understanding the variations in pocket price bands is critical to realizing a company's best transaction pricing opportunities. If a manager can identify a wide pocket price band and comprehend the underlying causes of the band's width, then he or she can manipulate that band to the company's benefit. Recall from Exhibit 1 the huge operating profit payoff from a 1% increase in average price. When, as in the case of the linoleum flooring manufacturer, pocket prices vary over a 35% range, it's not hard to imagine how more deliberate management of such wide price variations might yield several percentage points of price improvement—and the rich profit rewards that would accompany that improvement.

The width and shape of a pocket price band tell a fruitful story. Managers are invariably surprised not only by the width of their pocket price bands but also by the identity of customers at the extremes of the band. Customers perceived by managers as very profitable often end up at the low end of the band, and those perceived as unprofitable at the high end. The shape of the pocket price band provides the astute manager with a graphic profile of a business—depicting, among other things, what percentage of volume sells at deep discounts, whether there exist groups of customers who are willing to pay higher prices, and how appropriately field discounting authority is being exercised.

THE CASTLE BATTERY COMPANY CASE

The following, somewhat disguised, case shows how one company used the pocket price waterfall and band to identify profit leaks and regain control of its pricing system. It illustrates one way in which the waterfall and band concepts can be applied, and shows how, if a company doesn't manage its pricing policies on all levels, experienced customers may be working those policies to their own advantage.

The Castle Battery Company is a manufacturer of replacement lead-acid batteries for automobiles. Castle's direct customers are auto parts distributors, auto parts retailers, and some general mass merchandisers. With return on sales averaging in the 7% range, Castle's profitability is very sensitive to even small improvements in price: a 1% increase in price with no volume loss, for instance, would increase operating profit dollars by 14%.

Extreme overcapacity in the battery industry and gradual commoditization made it increasingly difficult for Castle to distinguish its products from competitors. So Castle senior management was skeptical that there was much, if any, potential for price improvement. But Castle managers had entirely overlooked lucrative pricing opportunities at the transaction level.

Exhibit 4 shows the typical pocket price waterfall for one of Castle's common battery models, the Power-Lite, sold to an auto parts retailer. From a base price of $28.40, Castle deducted standard dealer/distributor and order-size discounts. The company also subtracted an on-invoice exception discount, negotiated on a customer-by-customer basis to "meet competition." With these discounts, the invoice price to the retailer totaled $21.16. What little transaction price monitoring that Castle did focused exclusively on invoice.

That focus ignored a big part of the pricing picture—off-invoice discounting. Castle allowed cash discounts of 1.2% for timely payments by accounts. Additionally, the company granted extended terms (payment not required until 60 or 90 days after receipt of a shipment) as part of promotional programs or on an exception basis. For this

Exhibit 4. *Off-Invoice Discounts: A Big Part of the Pricing Picture*

(dollars per battery)

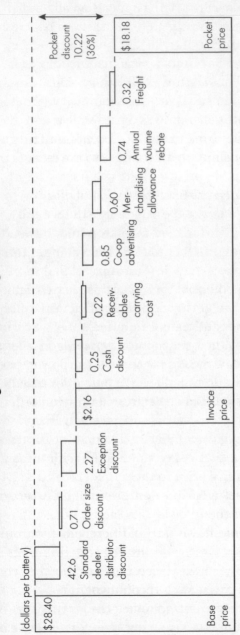

transaction, the extra cost of carrying these extended receivables totaled 22 cents. Cooperative advertising, where Castle contributed to its accounts' local advertising of Castle products, cost 85 cents. A special merchandising program in effect at the time of this transaction discounted another 60 cents. An annual volume rebate, based on total volume and paid at year end, decreased revenues by yet another 74 cents; and freight paid by Castle for shipping the battery to the retailer cost 32 cents.

The invoice price minus this long list of off-invoice items resulted in a pocket price of only $18.18, a full 14% less than invoice. The total revenue drop from base price down to pocket price is the "pocket discount"—in this case, $10.22, of which $2.98 was off-invoice.

Of course, not all transactions for this particular model of battery had the same pocket price. As Exhibit 5 shows, each element of the pocket price waterfall varied widely by customer and transaction, resulting in a very broad pocket price band. While the average pocket price was $20, units sold for as high as $25 and as low as $14—plus or minus greater than 25% around the average. A price band like this should trigger immediate questions: What are the underlying drivers of the band's shape and width? Why are pocket prices so variable, and can that variability be positively managed?

Castle managers were quite surprised at the width of the price band for their Power-Lite model, but on reflection, concluded that it was due to differences in account sizes. The company had a clear strategy of rewarding account volume with lower price, rationalizing that cost to serve would decrease with account volume.

But when management examined the Power-Lite pocket prices against total account sizes for a sample of

Exhibit 5. A Single Product Can Have a Wide Pocket Price Band

(Percent of volume)

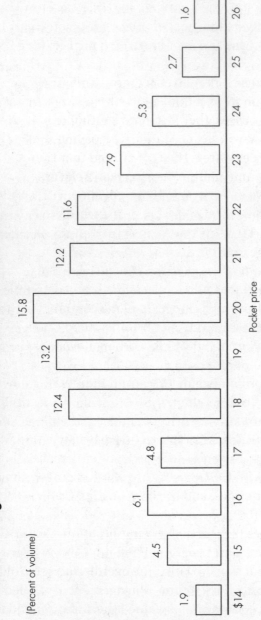

Pocket price

50 accounts, it found no correlation—it was a virtual shotgun blast. A number of relatively small accounts were buying at very low pocket prices while some very large accounts were buying at very high pocket price levels.

Castle managers, perplexed by the scatter of pocket prices by account size, launched an immediate investigation. In most cases, they found no legitimate reason why certain low-volume accounts were paying such discounted prices. Often, they discovered that these accounts were unusually experienced and clever accounts—customers who had been dealing with Castle for 20 years or more and who knew just whom to call at Castle headquarters to get that extra exception discount, that percentage point of additional co-op advertising, that extra 30 or 60 days to pay. These favorite old accounts were granted extra discounts based on familiarity and relationships rather than on economic justification. These experienced clients understood Castle's pocket price waterfall and were working it against the company.

Castle senior management realized that its transaction pricing process was out of control, that decision making up and down the waterfall lacked discipline, and that no one was focusing on the comprehensive total of those decisions. The end result was a pricing reality that didn't square with Castle's strategy of rewarding account size with lower prices, and that was costing Castle millions.

To correct its transaction pricing situation, Castle mounted a three-part program. First, it took very aggressive corrective actions to bring the overdiscounted, "old favorite" accounts back in line. Management identified the problem accounts and explained the situation and its

impact on overall company profits to the sales force.
Then the company gave the sales force nine months to
fix or drop those outliers. Fixing meant decreasing the
excessive discounting across the waterfall so that outlier
accounts' pocket prices were more in line with those of
accounts of similar size. Salespeople who couldn't negotiate their outlier pocket prices up to an appropriate
level were to find other accounts in their territory to
replace them.

Within the time allotted, the sales force fixed 90% of
the trouble accounts. Sales' newfound realization that
every element of the waterfall represented a viable negotiating lever contributed to this success. And, in most
cases, the salespeople easily found profitable replace-
ments for the other 10%.

Second, Castle launched a program to stimulate volume in larger accounts that had higher than average
pocket prices compared with accounts of similar size.
Management singled out the attractive "target" accounts
for special treatment. Sales and marketing personnel
investigated them carefully to determine the nonprice
benefits to which each was most sensitive. The company
increased volume in these accounts not by lowering price
but by delivering the specific benefits that were most
important to each: higher service levels for some, short-
ened order lead times for others, more frequent sales
calls for still others.

Finally, Castle embarked on a crash program to get
the transaction pricing process back under control. This
program included, among other components, setting
clear decision rules for each discretionary item in the
waterfall. For example, the company capped exception
discounts at 5% and granted them only after a specific
volume and margin impact evaluation. Management also

set up new information systems to guide and monitor transaction pricing decisions. And Castle established pocket price as the universal measure of price performance in all of these systems. It began to track and assign, transaction-by-transaction, all of the significant off-invoice waterfall elements that were previously collected and reported only on a companywide basis. Further, pocket price realization became a major component of the incentive compensation of salespeople, sales managers, and product managers.

Castle reaped rich and sustained rewards from these three transaction pricing initiatives. In the first year, average pocket price levels increased 3% and, even though volume remained flat, operating profits swelled 42%. The company realized additional pocket price gains in each of the two subsequent years.

Castle also received some unexpected strategic benefits from its newfound transaction pricing capability. Account-specific pocket price reporting revealed a small but growing distribution channel where Castle pocket prices were consistently higher than average. Increasing volume and penetration in this emerging channel became one of Castle's key strategic initiatives this past year. The fresh and more detailed business perspective that Castle senior managers gained from their transaction pricing involvement became the catalyst for an ongoing stream of similar strategic insights.

THE TECH-CRAFT COMPANY CASE

Consider another case—one that takes an even finer cut than the Castle example. Here, top management used both the pocket price waterfall and the pocket price band as broader tools. The company not only assimilated valuable information about its pricing policies but also used that knowledge to manipulate its pricing system and influence its retailers. The Tech-Craft Company took the waterfall and band and extended the concept, successfully applying the lessons of a financial tool to benefit its marketing strategy.

Tech-Craft is a manufacturer of home appliances, with microwave ovens as its primary line. Tech-Craft sells its microwave ovens directly to appliance retailers and a variety of mass merchandisers and department stores. With dozens of major and minor brands available, the microwave market is highly competitive and most retail outlets carry multiple brands.

Very complex price structures had evolved over the years in this competitive market. Exhibit 6 shows the average pocket price waterfall (on a percentage of dealer list price basis) for a Tech-Craft transaction to an appliance retailer. The company gave a total pocket discount of 39.1% over 11 different waterfall elements.

Research into competitors' pricing practices revealed that most competitors' price structures were just as complex as Tech-Craft's but varied in form—particularly off the invoice. For example, they varied by cash discount terms, co-op advertising rates, volume bonus discounts, volume break points, and freight payment policies. The variety and complexity of price structures made it somewhat difficult for appliance retailers to compare microwave prices among competitors. Further research showed that most retailers used just invoice price minus cash discount as their yardstick for comparing prices, taking for granted most of the off-invoice items. So a dollar discount on the invoice had much more impact on the retailer's buying decision than a dollar off the invoice.

Exhibit 6. Tech-Craft Gave a Pocket Discount of 39.1% After Waterfall Elements

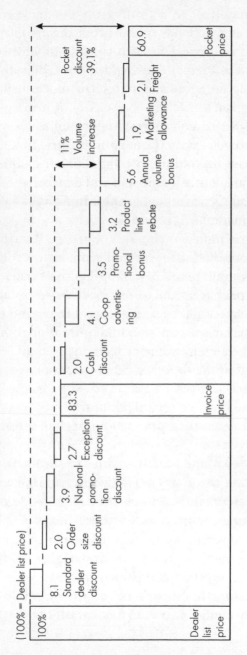

With this knowledge, Tech-Craft managers made a simple price structure change to one product line. They took their largest off-invoice discount—the annual volume bonus—and shifted it to on-invoice. To do this, they estimated each account's annual purchases at the beginning of the year, paid the volume bonus on the invoice based on that estimate, and then made an end-of-the-year adjustment if necessary. The result was an 11% increase in same-store volume, not by deeper discounting but rather by tailoring the pocket price waterfall so that Tech-Craft's price reflected the criterion that retailers used in comparing prices.

The result so intrigued Tech-Craft managers that they researched their pocket price waterfall even further, discovering evidence that retailers were not equally sensitive to price changes across all elements of the waterfall. For example, they found that retailers were much more sensitive to a $1 change in the national promotion discount than to a $1 change in the order-size discount, despite the fact that they affected Tech-Craft's pocket price equally. Tech-Craft managers used such insights regarding dealers' unequal sensitivity to different pieces of the waterfall to alter their pricing approach in several areas.

First, when they wanted to lower price to stimulate volume, Tech-Craft managers adjusted the waterfall elements to which their retailers were most sensitive—thus engendering the maximum volume growth. Conversely, when they wanted to raise price to increase margins, they adjusted the elements to which their retailers were least sensitive—thus minimizing loss of volume.

Second, over time they decreased the amount of discounting in the waterfall elements that just didn't matter to retailers, shifting part of that discounting to those elements that really influenced retailer buying decisions. By doing so, Tech-Craft made sure it was getting the most retailer buying preference for its discount dollars.

Tech-Craft management became quite skillful in the fine art of "waterfall engineering"—that is, fine-tuning the components of its pocket price waterfall to optimize the effect on buyer behavior. Not unlike Castle, Tech-Craft reaped rich rewards from its newfound skills and initiatives in transaction pricing. Within a year, the company had not only grown its unit volume by over 11% but also had increased average pocket price levels by 3.5%, resulting in a 60% operating profit improvement.

Capturing Untapped Transaction Pricing Opportunity

While the specific moves required to capture untapped transaction pricing opportunity can vary widely from company to company, the most useful improvement actions fall into three general areas.

1. MANAGE THE POCKET PRICE BAND

An understanding of pocket price and its variability across customers and transactions provides the bedrock of successful transaction price management. The entire pricing process should be managed toward pocket price realization rather than invoice price or list price. Pocket price should be the sole yardstick for determining the pricing attractiveness of products, customers, and individual deals. All price measurement and performance gauges should be recast with pocket price used as the base for calculating revenues. As the Castle Battery Company case demonstrates, considering business from this pocket price viewpoint can drastically change a company's perspective on the relative attractiveness of segments, customers, and transactions.

Creating information systems that correctly measure and report pocket price is problematic for many companies. Elements of the waterfall often reside on different systems or do not exist in data systems at all. These difficulties notwithstanding, companies should make the investment to produce a correct and comprehensive pocket price calculation. Managers must resist the temptation to leave elements out of the waterfall because they are difficult to calculate or inconvenient to include from an information systems standpoint. Effective transaction price management often requires tough customer initiatives, but incorrect or incomplete pocket price reporting gives managers an excuse not to initiate necessary pricing policies.

Once a company establishes a pocket price measure, it should drive explicit sales and marketing steps off the "tails" of the pocket price band. Excellent transaction pricers look to the pocket price band and target specific actions for the best and worst 10% to 20% of transactions and customers. Marketing and sales should target customers with transactions at the high end of the price band for increased volume. These departments should also identify clients at the low price end, marking them for actions that will either result in improved price levels or their termination as customers.

Management should not exclude any low-price customers, regardless of their history or relationship with the company, from such corrective actions. The hard pocket price numbers must determine which customers require remedial price action. Price band management initiatives quickly lose credibility and momentum if exceptions are made that allow favored customers to languish at the low end of a pocket price band.

2. ENGINEER THE POCKET PRICE WATERFALL

The best transaction pricers understand the leverage of waterfall engineering. Despite the fact that a dollar anywhere along the waterfall affects a company's pocket price and profit equally, the Tech-Craft case demonstrates that not all waterfall elements equally influence customer buying. A knowledge of which pieces of the waterfall matter to customers can guide not only how a company changes overall price and price structure but also how it negotiates with individual customers. Managers shouldn't be at all surprised if different sets of waterfall elements are important to different customer segments or different channels of distribution. Sales representative input can further enrich understanding of specific customer sensitivity to waterfall elements.

Each component of a company's pocket price waterfall deserves careful and explicit management. Top managers should set a quantifiable objective for each element of the pocket price waterfall, and if that goal is not achieved, they must change or even discontinue that element. Too many companies put in place a waterfall element like annual volume bonuses and leave it there unchanged, regardless of its effectiveness in influencing customer behavior. The sales and marketing organization should set hard objectives for each waterfall element. For example, the objective for an annual volume bonus might be to cause sales volume to grow at an average of 8% annually in existing accounts.

A company should take an annual snapshot of the results of its efforts. If it fails to meet its objective for a waterfall element, it should either adjust or eliminate that element. Excellent transaction pricing companies, like Tech-Craft, routinely reengineer their pocket price waterfalls and make each piece of the waterfall work for them.

3. GET ORGANIZATIONAL INVOLVEMENT AND INCENTIVES RIGHT

With percentage points of return on sales in the balance, transaction pricing merits broad organizational involvement; it is too important for even the president and CEO of a business to ignore. Companies that are best at transaction price management have general managers who understand its importance, set specific goals for transaction price improvement, and monitor those goals through regular and concise transaction price performance reports.

Exhibit 7 shows a quarterly "Pocket Price Source of Change" report that the president of Castle now uses to monitor the waterfall for major product lines. From it he can quickly see changes in average pocket price and understand the key sources of those changes along the price waterfall. He can recognize and reward pocket price improvement, question price performance shortfalls, and communicate to his organization that transaction pricing is important to him.

Deeper in the organization, superior transaction price performance seldom occurs unless top management offers appropriate incentives to key pricing influencers and decision makers like pricing managers, salespeople, sales managers, and marketing managers. Individuals incur an unavoidable risk when they strive for higher prices from customers—the risk of alienating the customer or losing the business altogether. It's always easier and less risky to price low. To offset the risk of pushing for higher price, tie incentives like compensation to pocket price realization.

Sales force incentives based on total sales revenue are not enough of an inducement for salespeople to push for higher prices. The pricing leverage for sales revenue-based compensation is always out of balance—

Exhibit 7. *A Quarterly Report Monitors the Waterfall for Major Product Lines*

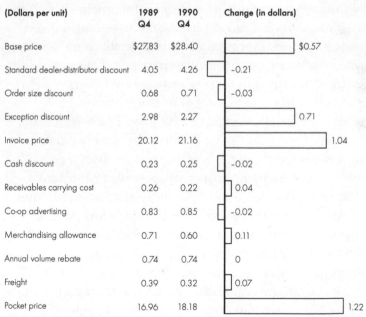

(Dollars per unit)	1989 Q4	1990 Q4	Change (in dollars)
Base price	$27.83	$28.40	$0.57
Standard dealer-distributor discount	4.05	4.26	-0.21
Order size discount	0.68	0.71	-0.03
Exception discount	2.98	2.27	0.71
Invoice price	20.12	21.16	1.04
Cash discount	0.23	0.25	-0.02
Receivables carrying cost	0.26	0.22	0.04
Co-op advertising	0.83	0.85	-0.02
Merchandising allowance	0.71	0.60	0.11
Annual volume rebate	0.74	0.74	0
Freight	0.39	0.32	0.07
Pocket price	16.96	18.18	1.22

a 5% decrease in price, for instance, will cause only a 5% decrease in a salesperson's compensation. But assuming average company economics, it will engender a 60% operating profit decrease for that transaction. Only sales incentive plans that abundantly reward above-average price realization and deeply penalize below average price levels will draw smart and profitable transaction price management from a sales force.

Even if salespeople have no explicit pricing authority, some sales force incentive for transaction price realization may still be prudent. Salespeople are usually the frontline negotiators and the carriers of a company's benefit and value message. They know the discounting limits their company will approve and will drop to those limits unless adequately compensated to do otherwise. The sales force role in transaction price management is simply too important for much progress to be made without their committed buy-in and support. In both the Castle and Tech-Craft cases, pocket price-based incentives for all pricing decision makers, including the sales force, fueled ongoing improvement in transaction pricing performance.

The transaction pricing opportunity is real and achievable for most companies today. The investment and risk of capturing this opportunity are low; the keys to success are mostly executional—doing a number of small things right. What is more, advances in information technology tend to make many of these small things easier than ever to do. And, as the Castle and Tech-Craft cases show, the payoff is extremely high, both in near-term and sustainable profit improvement and in valuable strategic insights. With its extremely favorable risk-effort-reward profile, improving transaction price man-

agement may be one of the most attractive and overlooked profit enhancement opportunities available to
most managers.

Notes

1. Arleigh W. Walker, "How to Price Industrial Products,"
   HBR September–October 1967, p. 125.

2. Elliot B. Ross, "Making Money with Proactive Pricing,"
   HBR November–December 1984, p. 145.

Originally published in September–October 1992
Reprint 92507

How to Fight a Price War

AKSHAY R. RAO, MARK E. BERGEN, AND
SCOTT DAVIS

Executive Summary

PRICE WARS ARE A FACT OF LIFE, whether we're talking about the fast-paced world of knowledge products,
the marketing of Internet appliances, or the staid, traditional sales of aluminum castings. If you're a manager
and you're not in battle currently, you probably will be
soon, so it's never too early to prepare.

The authors describe the causes and characteristics
of price wars and explain how companies can fight
them, flee them—or even start them. The authors say the
best defense in a pricing battle isn't to simply match price
cut for price cut; they emphasize other options for pro-
tecting market share.

For instance, companies can compete on quality
instead of price; they can alert customers to the risks and
negative consequences of choosing a low-priced option.
Companies can reveal their strategic intentions and

capabilities; just the threat of a major price action might hold rivals' pricing moves in check. And, finally, companies can seek support from interested third parties—governments, customers, and vendors, for instance—to help avert a price war.

If a company chooses to compete on price, the authors suggest using complex pricing actions, cutting prices in certain channels, or introducing new products or flanking brands—each of which lets companies selectively target only those segments of the market that are under competitive threat. A simple tit-for-tat price move should be the last resort—and managers should act swiftly and decisively so competitors will know that any revenue gains will be short-lived.

IN THE BATTLE TO CAPTURE the customer, companies use a wide range of tactics to ward off competitors. Increasingly, price is the weapon of choice—and frequently the skirmishing degenerates into a price war.

Creating low-price appeal is often the goal, but the result of one retaliatory price slashing after another is often a precipitous decline in industry profits. Look at the airline price wars of 1992. When American Airlines, Northwest Airlines, and other U.S. carriers went toe-to-toe in matching and exceeding one another's reduced fares, the result was record volumes of air travel—and record losses. Some estimates suggest that the overall losses suffered by the industry that year exceed the combined profits for the entire industry from its inception.

Price wars can create economically devastating and psychologically debilitating situations that take an extraordinary toll on an individual, a company, and industry profitability. No matter who wins, the combatants all seem to end up worse off than before they joined the battle. And yet, price wars are becoming increasingly common and uncommonly fierce. Consider the following two examples:

- In July 1999, Sprint announced a nighttime long-distance rate of 5 cents per minute. In August 1999, MCI matched Sprint's off-peak rate. Later that month, AT&T acknowledged that revenue from its consumer long-distance business was falling, and the company cut its long-distance rates to 7 cents per minute all day, everyday, for a monthly fee of $5.95. AT&T's stock dropped 4.7% the day of the announcement. MCI's stock price dropped 2.5%; Sprint's fell 3.8%.

- E-Trade and other electronic brokers are changing the competitive terrain of financial services with their extraordinarily low-priced brokerage services. The prevailing price for discount trades has fallen from $30 to $15 to $8 in the past few years.

There is little doubt, in the first example, that the major players in the long-distance phone business are in a price war. Price reductions, per-second billing, and free calls are the principal weapons the players bring to the competitive arena. There is little talk from any of the carriers about service, quality, brand equity, and other nonprice factors that might add value to a product or service. Virtually every competitive move is based on price, and every countermeasure is a retaliatory price cut.

In the second example, the competitive situation is subtly different—and yet still very much a price war. E-Trade's success demonstrates how the emergence of the Internet has fundamentally changed the cost of doing business. Consequently, even businesses such as Charles Schwab, which used to compete primarily on low-price appeal, are chanting a "quality" mantra. Meanwhile, Merrill Lynch and American Express have recognized that the emergence of the Internet will affect pricing and are changing their price structures to include free on-line trades for high-end customers. These companies appear to be engaged in more focused pricing battles, unlike the "globalized" price war in the long-distance phone market.

Most managers will be involved in a price war at some point in their careers. Every price cut is potentially the first salvo, and some discounts routinely lead to retaliatory price cuts that then escalate into a full-blown price war. That's why it's a good idea to consider other options before starting a price war or responding to an aggressive price move with a retaliatory one. Often, companies can avoid a debilitating price war altogether by using a set of alternative tactics. Our goal is to describe an arsenal of weapons other than price cuts that managers who are engaged in or contemplating a price war may also want to consider.

Take Inventory

Generally, price wars start because somebody somewhere thinks prices in a certain market are too high. Or someone is willing to buy market share at the expense of current margins. Price wars are becoming more common because managers tend to view a price change as an easy, quick, and reversible action. When businesses don't trust or know one another very well, the pricing battles can escalate very quickly. And whether they play out in the physical or the virtual world, price wars have a similar set of antecedents. By understanding their causes and characteristics, managers can make sensible decisions about when and how to fight a price war, when to flee one—and even when to start one.

The first step, then, is diagnosis. Consider a small commodities supplier that suddenly found that its largest competitor had slashed prices to a level well below the small company's costs. One option the smaller company considered was to lower its price in a tit-for-tat move. But that price would have been below the supplier's marginal cost; it would have suffered debilitating losses. Fortunately, a few phone calls revealed that its adversary was attempting to drive the supplier out of the local market by underpricing its products locally but maintaining high prices elsewhere. The supplier correctly diagnosed the pricing move as predatory and elected to do two things. First, the manager called customers in the competitor's home market to let them know that the price-cutter was offering special deals in another market. Second, he called local customers and asked them for their support, pointing out that if the smaller supplier was driven off the market, its customers would be facing a monopolist. The short-term price cuts would turn into long-term price hikes. The supplier identified solutions that eschewed further price cuts and thus averted a price war.

Intelligent analysis that leads to accurate diagnosis is more than half the cure. The process emphasizes understanding the opportunities for pricing actions based on current market trends and responding to competitors' actions based on the players and their resources. Not only is it necessary to understand why a price war is occurring or may occur, it also is critical to recognize where to look for the resources to do battle.

Good diagnoses involve analyzing four key areas in the theater of operations. They are *customer issues* such as price sensitivity and the customer segments that may emerge if prices change; *company issues* such as a business's cost structures, capabilities, and strategic positioning; *competitor issues,* such as a rival's cost structures, capabilities, and strategic positioning; and *contributor issues,* or the other players in the industry whose self-interest or profiles may affect the outcome of a price war. (For a more detailed explanation of such analyses, see the sidebar "Analyzing the Battleground" at the end of this article.)

Companies that step back and examine those four areas carefully often find that they actually have quite a few different options—including defusing the conflict, fighting it out on several fronts, or retreating. We'll look at some of those strategies and how companies have deployed them successfully.

Stop the War Before It Starts

There are several ways to stop a price war before it starts. One is to make sure your competitors understand the rationale behind your pricing policies. In other words, *reveal your strategic intentions.* Price-matching policies, everyday low pricing, and other public statements may communicate to competitors that you intend to fight a price war using all possible resources. But frequently these declarations about low prices, or about not engaging in price promotions, aren't low-price strategies at all. Such announcements are simply a way to tell competitors that you prefer to compete on dimensions other than price. When your competitors agree that such competition will be more profitable than competing on price, they'll tend to go along. That is precisely what happened when Winn-Dixie followed the Big Star supermarket chain in North Carolina and announced that it, too, would meet or beat mutual rival Food Lion's prices. After two years, the number of equipriced products among 79 commonly purchased brand items at the supermarkets had more than doubled. Further, the overall market price level had increased for these products. What happened? The stores stopped competing on price. In fact, the data

Ways to Fight a Price War

Tactic	Example
Nonprice Responses	
Reveal your strategic intentions and capabilities	Offer to match competitors' prices, offer everyday low pricing, or reveal your cost advantage
Compete on quality	Increase product differentiation by adding features to a product, or build awareness of existing features and their benefits. Emphasize the performance risks in low-priced options.
Co-opt contributors	Form strategic partnerships by offering cooperative or exclusive deals with suppliers, resellers, or providers of related services
Price Responses	
Use complex price actions	Offer bundled prices, two-part pricing, quantity discounts, price promotions, or loyalty programs for products
Introduce new products	Introduce flanking brands that compete in customer segments that are being challenged by competitors
Deploy simple price actions	Adjust product's regular price in response to a competitor's price change or another potential entry into the market

suggest that Food Lion raised its prices after its competitors announced they would match Food Lion's prices.

Making sure that your competitors know that your costs are low is another option—one that effectively warns them about the potential consequences of a price war. Hence it sometimes pays to *reveal your cost advantage.* Sara Lee has low variable costs, yet its products are relatively high priced compared with those of competitors. In the event of a price war, Sara Lee can drop its prices to levels that its competitors can't profitably match. The common knowledge about this low cost deters price cutting from competitors.

Sara Lee's management realizes that price cuts would be inconsistent with its strategic position of brand differentiation. Rather than use its low-cost structure to compete on price to build market share, Sara Lee uses its low costs as an implicit threat that helps prevent price wars. Essentially, a business that has relatively low variable costs enjoys an enviable advantage in a price war since competitors cannot sustain a price below their own variable costs in the long run. But low-cost companies should carefully consider their strategic positions before they start or join a price war. Lower costs often tempt a business to cut its prices, but doing so can diminish consumers' perceptions of quality and may trigger an unprofitable price war.

Responding with Nonprice Actions

Sometimes an analysis of the market reveals that several customer segments exhibit different degrees of sensitivity to price and quality. (See the sidebar "Price Sensitivity on the Web" at the end of this article for a look at how managers can identify and exploit differences in customers' price sensitivities—even in an information-rich environment.) Understanding the basis for certain customers' price sensitivities lets managers creatively respond to a rival's price cut without cutting their own prices. For example, a company might be able to *focus on quality, not price.*

Southeast Asia went through a rough time in 1997, particularly in the luxury product and service areas. The region's economy was unstable, Indonesian forest fires were wreaking havoc with the smog index, and tourism was clearly suffering. The economic turmoil dramatically reduced the value of the Malaysian ringgit to about half its value a few years earlier. The cost of a hotel room plummeted along with the nose-diving currency, yet hotel rooms went a-begging. What did the luxury hotel operators do to attract customers? They dropped their room rates even further. Luxury hotels in Malaysia entered a price war. All but one.

The Ritz-Carlton chose to steer clear of the fray. Instead, James McBride, the hotel's general manager, became creative. He greeted arriving flights with music, mimosas, discount coupons, and a model room. Passengers with reservations at other hotels began to defect to the Ritz at alarming rates. McBride provided his cellular phone number in newspaper ads so people could call him directly for reservations. Guests had round-the-clock access to a "technology butler" who could fix laptops and other electronic devices. The Ritz offered a "bath menu" of drinks and snacks to be served along with butler-drawn baths. Guests who stayed more than five nights received an embroidered pillowcase.

When luxury hotels start cutting their guest rates, their ability to offer "luxury" accoutrements drops. That means no fresh flowers, fewer towels, and a noticeable shortage of staff. But the Ritz kept its rates above 200 ringgit (about $52 U.S.) and was able to pay for low-cost services such as providing the embroidered pillowcases. Most important, the Ritz avoided any damage to its brand equity, something that could have easily occurred if typical Ritz customers arrived at the hotel and found it filled with noisy backpacking tourists or large families, all taking advantage of low prices. The negative spillover onto other Ritz properties could have been significant.

The Ritz-Carlton Kuala Lumpur last fall had no more empty rooms than its competitors; in fact, occupancy rates were up to 60% compared with a 50% occupancy rate in 1998. Perhaps most important, monthly gross operating profit on revenue of 2.2 million ringgit is about 400,000 ringgit—a return of about 18%.

Another way companies can avoid a price war is to *alert customers to risk*—specifically, the risk of poor quality. A senior product manager from the European operation of a large multinational pharmaceutical corporation lamented her recent pricing predicament. Her company's product, a medical diagnostic device, was the market-share leader, but a rival company had recently become aggressive on price. "They're crazy! Don't they see what they're doing to profits in the industry? Nobody can make money at these prices. What should I do? I've tried everything, and I can't get them to see the error of their ways," she said.

Not surprisingly, research confirmed that a large segment of customers in this "life and death" industry—doctors and testing laboratories—was quite risk averse and sensitive to variations in a product's performance. So rather than compete on price, the multinational appealed to customers' concerns about performance by emphasizing product enhancements such as improved reliability and greater detail in the information generated by the diagnostic device and by alerting buyers to the negative consequences of incomplete diagnoses. Some sales were lost to lower-priced products from the competitor, but the quality-sensitive segment allowed the multinational to maintain reasonable margins and avoid the negative spiral of a price war.

Federal Express provides another good example of how a company can appeal to performance sensitivity among customers. FedEx's brand equity exceeds that of virtually any company in the package delivery business. The shipping giant has built an enviable level of consumer recall and recognition through a highly effective advertising campaign. By emphasizing in ads and through other marketing efforts that a customer's package will "absolutely, positively" be there on time, FedEx plays on customers' risk aversion when dealing with time-sensitive documents.

A related weapon that companies can use to avert or battle a price war is to *emphasize other negative consequences.* The NutraSweet company employed this strategy when it faced the expiration of its patent. The company feared considerable price pressure from the producers of aspartame, the generic version of NutraSweet. A worst-case scenario would involve one of NutraSweet's major customers, such as Coca-Cola or Pepsi, switching to aspartame. If one of the companies switched, NutraSweet's contingency plan—which it shared with wavering Coke and Pepsi executives in Atlanta and New York—was a week-long advertising blitz that would alert consumers that "the other cola" was the only one that contained NutraSweet. Given the size of the market for carbonated soft drinks, NutraSweet's brand equity in the diet-conscious segment, and the potential short-term loss in market share and profits, this threat had teeth. NutraSweet successfully played one customer against another, emphasizing dire and unpalatable consequences, and thus averted a debilitating price war.

A final nonprice option involves *seeking help,* or appealing to contributors to weigh in on the competitive situation. For instance, when Sony entered the market for high-end imaging systems, the leaders in the imaging systems market in Belgium appealed to and received help from the central Belgian government. Not all companies can count on the government to come to their aid, of course. So companies might appeal to customers, vendors, channel partners, independent sales representatives, and other like-minded players if the price war could mean the company's demise. For instance, in the 1990s, Northwest Airlines appealed to its labor unions and received dramatic wage concessions so it could compete on price in a tight air-travel market.

Using Selective Pricing Actions

Employing complex options such as multiple-part pricing, quantity discounts, time-of-use pricing, bundling, and so on lets price warriors selectively cut rates for only those segments of the population that are under competitive threat.

One common—and classic—tactic is to *change customers' choices,* or reframe the price war in the minds of customers. McDonald's did it successfully when it faced Taco Bell's 59-cent taco strategy in the 1980s. By bundling burgers, fries, and drinks into "value meals," McDonald's reframed the price war from "tacos versus burgers" to "lunch versus lunch." Similarly, smart managers use quantity discounts or loyalty programs to insulate themselves from a price war. They avoid across-the-board price cuts, and they limit price reductions to areas in which they are vulnerable. In this way, managers can localize a price war to a limited theater of operation—and cut down the opportunities for the war to spill into other markets.

Therefore, another selective-pricing tactic might be to *modify only certain prices.* For instance, Sun Country Airlines, a discount carrier, entered Northwest's Minneapolis–St. Paul hub with 16 planes providing service to 14 cities. Sun Country's round-trip airfare to any location was generally low: Minneapolis to Boston was roughly $308. Rather than engage in a systemwide price cut, Northwest retained its existing fare structure with minor modifications. A Minneapolis–Boston round-trip was a relatively low $310 if tickets were purchased seven days in advance—but only for a flight that departed at 7:10 am and returned at 11:10 am. Curiously enough, Sun Country's only flight on that route departed Minneapolis at 7 am and Boston at 11:20 am. Northwest also employed several other resources, such as travel agents, to fend off Sun Country. Northwest reasoned that Sun Country did not have the infrastructure necessary to engage in an all-out price war and chose to not engage in any preemptive price cutting at times other than the flights directly affected. By targeting only certain fares for discounts, Northwest minimized internal changes but could still counter Sun Country's pricing ploy.

On another selective-pricing front, companies may use a *fighting brand.* In the early 1990s, Kao Corporation entered the diskette market with a low-priced product. Rather than drop its prices, 3M launched a flanking brand of low-priced diskettes called Highland because it knew that a large group of its customers was loyal to the

3M brand. Simply dropping the price on the 3M brand might have diluted 3M's quality image and its profits and may have stimulated further price cuts by Kao.

Because it understood its customers, 3M knew that many different segments of price-sensitive customers existed. Some people buy cheap diskettes, and some people don't care how much they pay for diskettes. More important, some people think cheap diskettes are probably of poor quality, and they may not buy them if the price is too low—perhaps because they are terrified of losing their data. 3M avoided the trap of charging what the market will bear. It recognized that markets will bear many prices, some better than others. That insight underpins the strategies of many software companies. For instance, marginally different versions of the same voice-recognition software can range in price from $79 to $8,000 depending on who the buyer is.[1]

You may not need a new brand to counter a price cut, just a new package. Consider the case of a major consumer-products company that faced an aggressive price-cutting competitor. The defending company finally dropped the price of its economy-size product with a "buy one, get one free" offer. Since the economy-size product lasts six months, the company took high-volume, price-sensitive users off the market for nearly a year. The resulting low sales of the competitor's product convinced the rival to cease and desist.

That illustration has several instructive elements to it. First, an acute understanding of the competitor's abilities, motives, and mind-set allowed the defending company to react effectively to a price war. Second, the expertise was complemented with a clear understanding of consumer behavior that allowed the company to prevent a price war. Third, the new entrant clearly picked the wrong adversary. The defending company was willing to suffer some losses (through cannibalization) in order to protect its turf.

Companies may also opt to *cut prices in certain channels.* Perhaps the single largest driver of price cuts and resulting price wars is excess capacity. The temptation to revive idle plants by stimulating demand through lower prices is often irresistible. But smart managers consider other options first. For instance, companies in the packaged-goods industry frequently sell off-brand or private-label versions of their national brands at low prices, ensuring that any price wars won't damage the brand equity of the national brands.

Similarly, airlines such as Delta are making a dent in reducing their unsold inventory by offering seats to consolidators and auction houses such as Priceline.com and Cheaptickets.com. The airlines are selling tickets to price-sensitive customers who don't care about flight times, number of stops, or frequent-flyer miles. Because the customer's point of contact is with the consolidator and not with the airline, the airline's image is protected—in much the same way that a nationally branded soup manufacturer protects its image by selling excess capacity under a private label.

But engaging in "stealth marketing" by selling low-priced, functionally equivalent alternatives through unrelated brand names or in foreign markets may still trigger price wars. If consumers recognize that the quality of the private-label product is comparable to that of the branded option, then the price of the branded option will need to drop. In many cases, it is best to leave plant capacity idle, since the attempt to revive it may trigger margin-destroying price competition. In fact, the idle capacity can be used as a weapon; a company then wields the credible threat of being able to flood the market with cheaper products should a competitor start cutting its prices.

Fight It Out

Although we feel strongly that direct, retaliatory price cuts should be a last resort, we do recognize that it is sometimes simply impossible to avoid a price war. Consider the case of personal computers. Expansion in this industry is occurring primarily at the low end as more and more price-sensitive consumers enter the market for PCs. EMachines, in Irvine, California, sells PCs that feature Intel's Celeron processor (a 366 MHz chip), a 4.3 gigabyte hard drive, and a host of other functions for roughly $400. High-profile brands such as HP and IBM are being forced to consider pricing their PCs in the $500 range to reach the first-time buyer. In this market, price cuts appear to be the only way to compete. In fact, "free PCs" are available to consumers who are willing to be exposed to a significant amount of advertising.

Clearly there are times when you must engage in a preemptive strike and start a price war—or respond to a competitor's discount with a matching or deeper price cut of your own. For instance, when a competitor threatens your core business, a retaliatory price cut can be used to signify your intention to fight long and hard. Similarly, when you can identify a large and growing segment of price-sensitive customers, when you have a cost advantage, when your pockets are deeper than competitors' pockets, when you can achieve economies of scale by expanding the market, or when a rival can be neutralized or eliminated because of high barriers to market entry and reentry, then engaging in price competition may be smart.

But there are several long-run implications of competing on price. First, a pattern of price cutting may teach customers to anticipate lower prices; more patient customers will defer their purchases until the next price cut. Second, a price-cutting company develops a reputation for being low-priced, and this reputation may cast doubt on the quality and image of other products under the umbrella brand and on the quality of future products. Third, price cuts have implications for other players in the market, whose self-interest may be harmed by lower prices.

If simple retaliatory price cuts are the chosen means of defense in a price war, then implement them quickly and unambiguously so competitors know that their sales gains from a price cut will be short-lived and monetarily unattractive. A slow response may prompt competitors to make additional price cuts in the future.

Retreat

On rare occasions, discretion is the better part of valor. Consequently, some businesses choose not to fight price wars; instead, they'll cede some market share rather than prolong a costly battle. 3M and DuPont are both companies that focus on developing innovations as part of their core strategy—and both have proved willing to cede share rather than participate in an unprofitable price war. In fact, 3M takes pride in the fact that roughly 40% of its revenue five years from now will come from new products. And in cases where it has retreated from pricing battles rather than standing its ground, the company seems to have come out ahead. For instance, because of withering price competition from high-volume, low-margin suppliers, 3M withdrew from the videotape business in the mid-1990s—even though videotape was invented at 3M. Similarly, Intel stopped manufacturing DRAM chips in the face of intense price competition from Taiwanese manufacturers in the 1980s, and its focus on processor chips has served it well. And Charles Schwab's decision to avoid a price war with low-priced Internet brokers has served stockholders well—the value of their Schwab holdings has more than quadrupled in the past two years.

It's Never Too Early to Prepare

It's in companies' best interests to reduce price competition because price wars can harm an entire industry. But diplomatic resolutions of price wars are generally impossible because overt diplomacy is a form of price collusion and may attract regulatory oversight. As a result, price leaders often engage in subtle forms of diplomacy that use market forces to discipline renegade companies that threaten industry profits.

Preventing a price war would be easy if it were possible to demonstrate the benefits of peace. Sadly, battle-scarred veterans who are suspicious of one another probably won't unilaterally disarm. So "price leadership" is one way to reduce industrywide price competition. Price leaders tend to develop reputations for eschewing price cuts as a way to gain market share and for responding quickly and decisively to price cutting by renegade companies. The price leaders are viewed as credible enforcers of price regimes based on their cost structures, strategic postures, or the personal characteristics of their officers. We do caution, however, that a pattern of disciplinary moves may attract unwelcome regulatory scrutiny; companies should carefully consider whether their attempts at exercising leadership may be interpreted as anticompetitive.

Price wars are a fact of life—whether we're talking about the fast-paced world of "knowledge products," the marketing of Internet appliances, or the staid, traditional business of aluminum castings. If you are not in battle currently, you probably will be fairly soon, so it's never too early to prepare.

If you are currently in a price war, understand that you can use several nonprice options to defend yourself and recognize that it is sometimes best to cede the turf under contention and seek greener pastures. If the current combatants can't be vanquished, it may be wise to observe the price war from the sidelines and enter the fray after everyone else has been eviscerated. Sometimes, to the bystanders go the spoils of war.

Analyzing the Battleground

IT'S NECESSARY TO UNDERSTAND why a price war is occurring—or may occur. But it's also critical to recognize where to look for resources in battle. It's important to carefully analyze your customers, company, competitors, and other players within and outside the industry that may have an interest in how the price war plays out.

Customers and Price Sensitivity

A thoughtful evaluation of customers and their price sensitivities can provide valuable insights about whether one should fight a competitor's price cut with a price cut in kind or with some other strategy. Consumers are frequently unaware of substitute products and their prices, or they may find it difficult to make comparisons among functionally equivalent alternatives. For instance, prior to AT&T's 7-cents-a-minute plan, consumers faced a bewildering set of pricing options for long-distance phone service. AT&T charged 15 cents per minute per call with no monthly fee; or 10 cents per minute with a $4.95 monthly fee. MCI offered nighttime rates of 5 cents a minute, daytime rates of up to 25 cents a minute, and a monthly fee of $1.95. Sprint charged 5 cents per minute for nighttime calls, rates of up to 10 cents per minute for other calls, and a $5.95 monthly fee. The cost of determining the best plan when customers are unsure about their calling patterns is simply too high for a low-involvement decision like long-distance phone service. A company that wanted to compete on price could choose to simplify. That's exactly what Sprint did. It simplified its price schedule to 10 cents a minute so customers could compare its rates to those from MCI and AT&T.

Some consumers are more sensitive to quality than price, for a variety of reasons. Industrial buyers are often willing to pay more for on-time delivery or consistent quality because they need those features to make their businesses run smoother and more profitably. The very rational belief that poor quality can endanger one's health is an important reason that branded drugs command the prices they do relative to generic drugs. And snob appeal allows Davidoff to sell matches at $3.25 for a box of 40 sticks to cigar connoisseurs. The basic lesson is that different customer segments exhibit different levels of price sensitivity for different products at different times. Businesses that adopt a one-size-fits-all approach to pricing do so at their peril.

Company Abilities

Company factors such as cost structures, capabilities, and strategic positioning should also be examined carefully. Cost structures may be affected by changes in technology or business practices, which in turn may tempt a company to cut prices in a manner that will trigger a price war. For example, consider the implications of outsourcing. It's probably true that it is cheaper to buy rather than make something in-house, because the invisible hand of the marketplace will lower the acquisition price of a product. But the cost of manufacturing something in-house is largely sunk and fixed. When that product is purchased on the market, its acquisition cost is a variable one. In other words, integration can lead to a cost structure with a higher fixed-cost component and a lower variable-cost component. Consequently, the company with the lower variable costs may be tempted to reduce prices and start a price war. But even though the lower variable costs give the company an advantage, it should carefully consider whether a price war is consistent with its strategic posture. The company's lower variable costs should be used to start a price war only when it will result in the neutralization or the exit of an undesirable rival.

Consider, too, the coherence of your pricing strategy and your ability to execute it. The actions of one participant engaged in a fierce price war in the utility industry is telling: The company's senior management group asked its top manager to increase market share by 20%, return prices to profitable levels, and stabilize them. Confronted with apparently conflicting goals, the manager chose the easiest goal—build market share—which he achieved by lowering prices, thus exacerbating the price war. The directive to the manager was confusing, his resulting actions baffled competitors, and that led to considerable uncertainty and increased price turbulence in the market. When the soft costs (managerial time and attention) of changing prices through a complex supply chain were factored in, the cost of the increased market share was very dear.

The essential insight that should emerge from this exercise is whether a simple price cut is the best option given one's cost structure, capacity levels, and organizational competence.

Competitors' Response

An analysis of competitors—their cost structures, capabilities, and strategic positioning—is equally valuable. Industrywide price reductions may be appropriate under certain circumstances. But many unprofitable price wars happen because a company sees an opportunity to increase market share or profits through lower prices, while ignoring the fact that competitors will respond. Market research may reveal that sales increases following a price cut justify the action, but this same research often simply ignores competitors' price responses.

Businesses need to pay attention at the strategic level to the twin questions of who will respond and how. Smart product managers recognize the need to understand the competition and empathize with them. They project how competitors will set prices by carefully tracking historical patterns, understanding which events have triggered price changes in the past, and by tracking the timing and magnitude of price responses. They monitor public statements made by senior executives and published in company reports. And they keep their eyes peeled for activity in resource markets: competitors that acquire a new technology, labor force, information system, or distribution channel, or that form a new brand alliance, will probably make some kind of a price move that will affect other players in the industry. This sophisticated environmental scanning identifies possible adversaries and their likely modus operandi.

But which competitors should you watch? Identifying competitors often has important pricing implications. For instance, Encyclopedia Britannica discovered that its chief rival is not Grolier's Encyclopedia but Microsoft. Britannica seemed oblivious to this important competitor for several years until a steady erosion in encyclopedia sales alerted the company to startling developments in technology that changed the way consumers get information. Its books once costs thousands of dollars; Britannica now offers free access to its database on the Web and derives its revenues from banner ads, not consumers.

A company's direct competitors that share the same technology and speak to the same markets are important rivals. But indirect competitors that satisfy customer needs through the use of different technologies and that have completely different cost structures are perhaps the most dangerous. In fact, direct competitors such as major airlines frequently coexist quite peacefully. Examining their pricing-decision rules suggests why. U.S. Department of Transportation studies indicate that when one hub-based airline enters another's hub, it typically does not engage in price-based competition because it fears retaliation in its own hub. Conversely, price wars may often be started by a company from an entirely different industry, with a radically different technology, whose cost advantages give it enough leverage to enter your market and steal your share.

The process of identifying competitors also reveals the strengths and weaknesses of current and potential rivals. This has important implications for how a company competes. It is generally wise to not stir a hornet's nest by starting a price war with a competitor that has a significantly larger resource base or a reputation for being a fierce price warrior. When analyzing your competition, carefully determine who they are, how price fits with their

strategic position, how they make pricing decisions, and
what their capabilities and resources are.

Contributors, Collaborators, and Other Interested Parties

Finally, it is important to monitor other players in the industry whose self-interest or profiles may affect outcomes.
Suppliers, distributors, providers of complementary
goods and services, customers, government agencies,
and so on contribute significantly to the consumption
experience, including product quality, the sales pitch,
and after-sales service. They often wield considerable
influence on the outcome of a price war—directly or
indirectly. Sometimes these contributors may provide the
impetus for, or may indirectly start, a price war. Motorola
discovered as much when it introduced low-priced
cellular phones in China and Brazil. Soon Motorola
observed that the street price for its phones had dropped
substantially in the United States. Distributors were divert-
ing products bound for China and Brazil to the profitable
U.S. and European markets; sometimes the products
never even left the dock. Motorola's distributors had created a "gray market" because Motorola had given them
a reason to believe that prices in the United States were
too high.

Sometimes contributors can help reduce price competition by enhancing the product's value, as Intel does
for computer manufacturers; assisting with marketing, as
airline frequent-flyer programs do for credit-card companies; and limiting the exposure to competing products, as
MITI has done for Japanese companies facing international competition at home. Smart managers must carefully consider other players and their interests (profit margins for suppliers and distributors, commissions for sales

representatives, and so on) before starting a price war or joining one.

Price Sensitivity on the Web

INTERNET COMPANIES SUCH AS Buy.com are attempting to build market share by charging low prices. They operate under the premise that Internet shoppers are extremely sensitive to price. But the evidence to back up that assumption is mixed. On the one hand, the Web offers an easy way to search and compare prices. On the other hand, on-line shoppers tend to search for quality attributes, as well. Professors John G. Lynch of Duke University's Fuqua School of Business and Dan Ariely of MIT's Sloan School of Management have recently demonstrated that making quality information more accessible on the Web reduces price sensitivity.[1] That is why Amazon.com can charge higher prices than other on-line sites. The variety of titles it offers, the extensive product information it provides, and its reputation for rapid and reliable shipping make Amazon an easy choice for consumers who want convenience and low prices.

The growth of Internet shopping is posing interesting pricing dilemmas for bricks-and-mortar retailers. On-line vendors don't have to maintain a physical presence close to their customers, so they can operate out of a few large warehouses, thus lowering their costs. It would generally be unwise for bricks-and-mortar retailers to try to compete on price given the relatively high cost of maintaining a storefront. Instead, their strategy should emphasize features that can't be provided over the

Web, such as personalized face-to-face service, browsing, immediate delivery, low-hassle returns and exchanges that don't require repackaging and shipping, and the ability to touch the product. Several retailers, such as Barnes & Noble and Tower Records, have developed an Internet presence to complement their storefronts. Such "clicks and mortar" retailers give customers the option to purchase or order on-line and then pick up the product at a bricks-and-mortar branch, and those retailers often provide a search engine in the store that is similar to their Internet offerings.

Finally, a keen understanding of consumer behavior lets some companies charge higher prices on the Web because of the anonymity that on-line transactions offer. In a recent study of 46 e-tailers of prescription drugs, the two most popular items (Viagra, a medication for erectile dysfunction, and Propecia, a medication to treat male pattern baldness) were priced roughly 10% higher than in drug stores. For obvious reasons, people prefer to have those prescriptions filled without personal contact and are willing to pay a premium for a faceless transaction.

1. See "Wine Online: Search Costs and Competition on Price, Quality, and Distribution," Marketing Science, 2000.

Notes

1. See Carl Shapiro and Hal Varian, "Versioning: The Smart Way to Sell Information," HBR November–December 1998.

Originally published in March–April 2000
Reprint R00208

Pricing Policies for New Products

JOEL DEAN

Executive Summary

HBR FIRST PUBLISHED this article in November 1950 as a practical guide to the problems involved in pricing new products. Particularly in the early stages of competition, it is necessary to estimate demand, anticipate the effect of various possible combinations of prices, and choose the most suitable promotion policy. Then as the product's market status matures, policy revisions become necessary. Joel Dean outlines the possible price strategies for each stage of a product's market evolution and the various grounds for making a choice. To update his original statement, Mr. Dean has written a retrospective comment, which appears at the end of this article. He amplifies his earlier article with insights from intervening years and in light of such developments as inflation.

How to price a new product is a top management puzzle that is too often solved by cost-theology and hunch. This article suggests a pricing policy geared to the dynamic nature of a new product's competitive status. Today's high rate of innovation makes the economic evolution of a new product a strategic guide to practical pricing.

New products have a protected distinctiveness which is doomed to progressive degeneration from competitive inroads. The invention of a new marketable specialty is usually followed by a period of patent protection when markets are still hesitant and unexplored and when product design is fluid. Then comes a period of rapid expansion of sales as market acceptance is gained.

Next the product becomes a target for competitive encroachment. New competitors enter the field, and innovations narrow the gap of distinctiveness between the product and its substitutes. The seller's zone of pricing discretion narrows as his or her distinctive "specialty" fades into a pedestrian "commodity" which is so little differentiated from other products that the seller has limited independence in pricing, even if rivals are few.

Throughout the cycle, continual changes occur in promotional and price elasticity and in costs of production and distribution. These changes call for adjustments in price policy.

Appropriate pricing over the cycle depends on the development of three different aspects of maturity, which usually move in almost parallel time paths:

1. Technical maturity, indicated by declining rate of product development, increasing standardization

among brands, and increasing stability of manufacturing processes and knowledge about them.

2. Market maturity, indicated by consumer acceptance of the basic service idea, by widespread belief that the products of most manufacturers will perform satisfactorily, and by enough familiarity and sophistication to permit consumers to compare brands competently.

3. Competitive maturity, indicated by increasing stability of market shares and price structures.

Of course, interaction among these components tends to make them move together. That is, intrusion by new competitors helps to develop the market, but entrance is most tempting when the new product appears to be establishing market acceptance.

The rate at which the cycle of degeneration progresses varies widely among products. What are the factors that set its pace? An overriding determinant is technical—the extent to which the economic environment must be reorganized to use the innovation effectively. The scale of plant investment and technical research called forth by the telephone, electric power, the automobile, or air transport makes for a long gestation period, as compared with even such major innovations as cellophane or frozen foods.

Development comes fastest when the new gadget fills a new vacuum made to order for it. Electric stoves, as one example, rose to 50% market saturation in the fast-growing Pacific Northwest, where electric power had become the lowest-cost energy.

Products still in early developmental stages also provide rich opportunities for product differentiation, which with heavy research costs holds off competitive degeneration.

But aside from technical factors, the rate of degeneration is controlled by economic forces that can be subsumed under rate of market acceptance and ease of competitive entry.

Market acceptance means the extent to which buyers consider the product a serious alternative to other ways of performing the same service. Market acceptance is a frictional factor. The effect of cultural lags may endure for some time after quality and costs make products technically useful. The slow catch-on of the garbage-disposal unit is an example.

On the other hand, the attitude of acceptance may exist long before any workable model can be developed; then the final appearance of the product will produce an explosive growth curve in sales. The antihistamine cold tablet, a spectacular example, reflected the national faith in chemistry's ability to vanquish the common cold. And, of course, low unit price may speed market acceptance of an innovation; ballpoint pens and all-steel houses started at about the same time, but look at the difference in their sales curves.

Ease of competitive entry is a major determinant of the speed of degeneration of a specialty. An illustration is found in the washing machine business before the war, where with little basic patent protection the Maytag position was quickly eroded by small manufacturers who performed essentially an assembly operation. The ballpoint pen cascaded from a $12 novelty to a 49-cent "price football," partly because entry barriers of patents and techniques were ineffective. Frozen orange juice, which started as a protected specialty of Minute Maid, sped through its competitive cycle, with competing brands crowding into the market.

At the outset innovators can control the rate of competitive deterioration to an important degree by nonprice as well as by price strategies. Through successful research in product improvement innovators can protect their specialty position both by extending the life of their basic patents and by keeping ahead of competitors in product development. The record of IBM punch-card equipment is one illustration. Ease of entry is also affected by a policy of stay-out pricing (so low as to make the prospects look uninviting), which under some circumstances may slow down the process of competitive encroachment.

Steps in Pioneer Pricing

Pricing problems start when a company finds a product that is a radical departure from existing ways of performing a service and that is temporarily protected from competition by patents, secrets of production, control at the point of a scarce resource, or by other barriers. The seller here has a wide range of pricing discretion resulting from extreme product differentiation.

A good example of pricing latitude conferred by protected superiority of product was provided by the McGraw Electric Company's "Toastmaster," which, both initially and over a period of years, was able to command a very substantial price premium over competitive toasters. Apparently this advantage resulted from (1) a good product that was distinctive and superior and (2) substantial and skillful sales promotion.

Similarly, Sunbeam priced its electric iron $2 above comparable models of major firms with considerable success. And Sunbeam courageously priced its new metal coffeemaker at $32, much above competitive makes of glass coffeemakers, but it was highly successful.

To get a picture of how a manufacturer should go about setting a price in the pioneer stage, let me describe the main steps of the process (of course the classification is arbitrary and the steps are interrelated): (1) estimate of demand, (2) decision on market targets, (3) design of promotional strategy, and (4) choice of distribution channels.

ESTIMATE OF DEMAND

The problem at the pioneer stage differs from that in a relatively stable monopoly because the product is beyond the experience of buyers and because the perishability of its distinctiveness must be reckoned with. How can demand for new products be explored? How can we find out how much people will pay for a product that has never before been seen or used? There are several levels of refinement to this analysis.

The initial problem of estimating demand for a new product can be broken into a series of subproblems: (1) whether the product will go at all (assuming price is in a competitive range), (2) what range of price will make the product economically attractive to buyers, (3) what sales volumes can be expected at various points in this price range, and (4) what reaction will price produce in manu-facturers and sellers of displaced substitutes.

The first step is an exploration of the *preferences and educability of consumers,* always, of course, in the light of the technical feasibility of the new product. How many potential buyers are there? Is the product a practical device for meeting their needs? How can it be improved to meet their needs better? What proportion of the potential buyers would prefer, or could be induced to prefer, this product to already existing products (prices being equal)?

Sometimes it is feasible to start with the assumption that all vulnerable substitutes will be fully displaced. For example, to get some idea of the maximum limits of demand for a new type of reflecting-sign material, a company started with estimates of the aggregate number and area of auto license plates, highway markers, railroad operational signs, and name signs for streets and homes. Next, the proportion of each category needing night-light reflection was guessed. For example, it was assumed that only rural and suburban homes could benefit by this kind of name sign, and the estimate of need in this category was made accordingly.

It is not uncommon and possibly not unrealistic for a manufacturer to make the blithe assumption at this stage that the product price will be "within a competitive range" without having much idea of what that range is. For example, in developing a new type of camera equipment, one of the electrical companies judged its acceptability to professional photographers by technical performance without making any inquiry into its economic value. When the equipment was later placed in an economic setting, the indications were that sales would be negligible.

The second step is marking out this *competitive range of price*. Vicarious pricing experience can be secured by interviewing selected distributors who have enough comparative knowledge of customers' alternatives and preferences to judge what price range would make the new product "a good value." Direct discussions with representative experienced industrial users have produced reliable estimates of the "practical" range of prices. Manufacturers of electrical equipment often explore the economic as well as the technical feasibility of a new product by sending engineers with blueprints and models to see customers, such as technical and operating executives.

In guessing the price range of a radically new consumers' product of small unit value, the concept of barter equivalent can be a useful research guide.

For example, a manufacturer of paper specialties tested a dramatic new product in the following fashion: A wide variety of consumer products totally unlike the new product were purchased and spread out on a big table. Consumers selected the products they would swap for the new product. By finding out whether the product would trade evenly for a dish pan, a towel, or a hairpin, the executives got a rough idea of what range of prices might strike the typical consumer as reasonable in the light of the values received for his or her money in totally different kinds of expenditures.

But asking prospective consumers how much they think they would be willing to pay for a new product, even by such indirect or disguised methods, may often fail to give a reliable indication of the demand schedule. Most times people just do not know what they would pay. It depends partly on their income and on future alternatives. Early in the postwar period a manufacturer of television sets tried this method and got highly erratic and obviously unreliable results because the distortion of war shortages kept prospects from fully visualizing the multiple ways of spending their money.

Another deficiency, which may, however, be less serious than it appears, is that responses are biased by the consumer's confused notion that he or she is bargaining for a good price. Not until techniques of depth interviewing are more refined than they are now can this crude and direct method of exploring a new product's demand schedule hold much promise of being accurate.

One appliance manufacturer tried out new products on a sample of employees by selling to them at deep dis-

counts, with the stipulation that they could if they
wished return the products at the end of the experiment
period and get a refund of their low purchase price.
Demand for foreign orange juice was tested by placing it
in several markets at three different prices, ranging
around the price of fresh fruit; the result showed rather
low price elasticity.

While inquiries of this sort are often much too short-
run to give any real indication of consumer tastes, the
relevant point here is that even such rough probing often
yields broad impressions of price elasticity, particularly
in relation to product variations such as styling, placing
of controls, and use of automatic features. It may show,
for example, that $5 of cost put into streamlining or
chromium stripping can add $50 to the price.

The third step, a more definite inquiry into the *probable sales from several possible prices,* starts with an investigation of the prices of substitutes. Usually the buyer
has a choice of existing ways of having the same service
performed; an analysis of the costs of these choices
serves as a guide in setting the price for a new way.

Comparisons are easy and significant for industrial
customers who have a costing system to tell them the
exact value, say, of a forklift truck in terms of warehouse
labor saved. Indeed, chemical companies setting up a
research project to displace an existing material often
know from the start the top price that can be charged
for the new substitute in terms of cost of the present
material.

But in most cases the comparison is obfuscated by the
presence of quality differences that may be important
bases for price premiums. This is most true of house-
hold appliances, where the alternative is an unknown
amount of labor of a mysterious value. In pricing a cargo

parachute the choices are: (1) free fall in a padded box from a plane flown close to the ground, (2) landing the plane, (3) back shipment by land from the next air terminal, or (4) land shipment all the way. These options differ widely in their service value and are not very useful pricing guides.

Thus it is particularly hard to know how much good will be done by making the new product cheaper than the old by various amounts, or how much the market will be restricted by making the new product more expensive. The answers usually come from experiment or research.

The fourth step in estimating demand is to consider the *possibility of retaliation by manufacturers of displaced substitutes* in the form of price cutting. This development may not occur at all if the new product displaces only a small market segment. If old industries do fight it out, however, their incremental costs provide a floor to the resulting price competition and should be brought into price plans.

For example, a manufacturer of black-and-white sensitized paper studied the possibility that lowering its price would displace blueprint paper substantially. Not only did the manufacturer investigate the prices of blueprint paper, but it also felt it necessary to estimate the out-of-pocket cost of making blueprint paper because of the probability that manufacturers already in the market would fight back by reducing prices toward the level of their incremental costs.

DECISION ON MARKET TARGETS

When the company has developed some idea of the range of demand and the range of prices that are feasible for the new product, it is in a position to make some basic strategic decisions on market targets and promotional plans. To decide on market objectives requires answers to several questions: What ultimate market share is wanted for the new product? How does it fit into the present product line? What about production methods? What are the possible distribution channels?

These are questions of joint costs in production and distribution, of plant expansion outlays, and of potential competition. If entry is easy, the company may not be eager to disrupt its present production and selling operations to capture and hold a large slice of the new market. But if the prospective profits shape up to a substantial new income source, it will be worthwhile to make the capital expenditures on plant needed to reap the full harvest.

A basic factor in answering all these questions is the expected behavior of production and distribution costs. The relevant data here are all the production outlays that will be made after the decision day—the capital expenditures as well as the variable costs. A go-ahead decision will hardly be made without some assurance that these costs can be recovered before the product becomes a football in the market. Many different projections of costs will be made, depending on the alternative scales of output, rate of market expansion, threats of potential competition, and measures to meet that competition that are under consideration. But these factors and the decision that is made on promotional strategy are interdependent. The fact is that this is a circular problem that in theory can only be solved by simultaneous equations.

Fortunately, it is possible to make some approximations that can break the circle: scale economies become significantly different only with broad changes in the size of plant and the type of production methods. This narrows the range of cost projections to workable proportions. The effects of using different distribution channels can be guessed fairly well without meshing the choices in with all the production and selling possibilities. The most vulnerable point of the circle is probably the decision on promotional strategy. The choices here are broad and produce a variety of results. The next step in the pricing process is therefore a plan for promotion.

DESIGN OF PROMOTIONAL STRATEGY

Initial promotion outlays are an investment in the product that cannot be recovered until some kind of market has been established. The innovator shoulders the burden of creating a market—educating consumers to the existence and uses of the product. Later imitators will never have to do this job; so if the innovator does not want to be simply a benefactor to future competitors, he or she must make pricing plans to recover initial outlays before his or her pricing discretion evaporates.

The innovator's basic strategic problem is to find the right mixture of price and promotion to maximize long-run profits. He or she can choose a relatively high price in pioneering stages, together with extravagant advertising and dealer discounts, and plan to recover promotion costs early; or he or she can use low prices and lean margins from the very outset in order to discourage potential competition when the barriers of patents, distribution channels, or production techniques become inadequate. This question is discussed further later on.

CHOICE OF DISTRIBUTION CHANNELS

Estimation of the costs of moving the new product through the channels of distribution to the final consumer must enter into the pricing procedure, since these costs govern the factory price that will result in a specified consumer price and since it is the consumer price that matters for volume. Distributive margins are partly pure promotional costs and partly physical distribution costs. Margins must at least cover the distributors' costs of warehousing, handling, and order taking. These costs are similar to factory production costs in being related to physical capacity and its utilization, i.e., fluctuations in production or sales volume.

Hence these set a floor to trade-channel discounts. But distributors usually also contribute promotional effort—in point-of-sale pushing, local advertising, and display—when it is made worth their while.

These pure promotional costs are more optional. Unlike physical handling costs they have no necessary functional relation to sales volume. An added layer of margin in trade discounts to produce this localized sales effort (with retail price fixed) is an optional way for manufacturers to spend their prospecting money in putting over a new product.

In establishing promotional costs, manufacturers must decide on the extent to which the selling effort will be delegated to members of the distribution chain. Indeed, some distribution channels, such as house-to-house selling and retail store selling supplemented by home demonstrators, represent a substantial delegation of the manufacturers' promotional efforts, and these usually involve much higher distribution-channel costs than do conventional methods.

Rich distributor margins are an appropriate use of promotion funds only when the producer thinks a high price plus promotion is a better expansion policy in the specialty than low price by itself. Thus there is an intimate interaction between the pricing of a new product

and the costs and the problems of floating it down the
distribution channels to the final consumer.

Policies for Pioneer Pricing

The strategic decision in pricing a new product is the
choice between (1) a policy of high initial prices that
skim the cream of demand and (2) a policy of low prices
from the outset serving as an active agent for market
penetration. Although the actual range of choice is much
wider than this, a sharp dichotomy clarifies the issues for
consideration.

SKIMMING PRICE

For products that represent a drastic departure from
accepted ways of performing a service, a policy of relatively high prices coupled with heavy promotional
expenditures in the early stages of market development
(and lower prices at later stages) has proved successful
for many products. There are several reasons for the success of this policy:

1. Demand is likely to be more inelastic with respect to
   price in the early stages than it is when the product is
   full grown. This is particularly true for consumers'
   goods. A novel product, such as the electric blanket
   when it first came out, was not accepted early on
   as a part of the expenditure pattern. Consumers
   remained ignorant about its value compared with
   the value of conventional alternatives. Moreover, at
   least in the early stages, the product had so few close
   rivals that cross-elasticity of demand was low.

Promotional elasticity is, on the other hand, quite high, particularly for products with high unit prices such as television sets. Since it is difficult for customers to value the service of the product in a way to price it intelligently, they are by default principally interested in how well it will work.

2. Launching a new product with a high price is an efficient device for breaking the market up into segments that differ in price elasticity of demand. The initial high price serves to skim the cream of the market that is relatively insensitive to price. Subsequent price reductions tap successively more elastic sectors of the market. This pricing strategy is exemplified by the systematic succession of editions of a book, starting with a very expensive limited personal edition and ending up with a much lower-priced paperback.

3. This policy is safer, or at least appears so. Facing an unknown elasticity of demand, a high initial price serves as a "refusal" price during the stage of exploration. It is difficult to predict how much costs can be reduced as the market expands and as the design of the product is improved by increasing production efficiency with new techniques. When an electrical company introduced a new lamp bulb at a comparatively high initial price, it made the announcement that the price would be reduced as the company found ways of cutting its costs.

4. Many companies are not in a position to finance the product flotation out of distant future revenues. High cash outlays in the early stages result from heavy costs of production and distributor organizing, in

addition to the promotional investment in the pioneer product. High prices are a reasonable financing technique for shouldering these burdens in the light of the many uncertainties about the future.

PENETRATION PRICE

The alternative policy is to use low prices as the principal instrument for penetrating mass markets early. This policy is the reverse of the skimming policy in which the price is lowered only as short-run competition forces it.

The passive skimming policy has the virtue of safeguarding some profits at every stage of market penetration. But it prevents quick sales to the many buyers who are at the lower end of the income scale or the lower end of the preference scale and who therefore are unwilling to pay any substantial premium for product or reputation superiority. The active approach in probing possibilities for market expansion by early penetration pricing requires research, forecasting, and courage.

A decision to price for market expansion can be reached at various stages in a product's life cycle: before birth, at birth, in childhood, in adulthood, or in senescence. The chances for large-volume sales should at least be explored in the early stages of product development research, even before the pilot stage, perhaps with a more definitive exploration when the product goes into production and the price and distribution plans are decided upon. And the question of pricing to expand the market, if not answered earlier, will probably arise once more after the product has established an elite market.

Quite a few products have been rescued from premature senescence by being priced low enough to tap new markets. The reissues of important books as lower-priced paperbacks illustrate this point particularly well. These have produced not only commercial but intellectual renascence as well to many authors. The patterns of sales growth of a product that had reached stability in a high-price market have undergone sharp changes when it was suddenly priced low enough to tap new markets.

A contrasting illustration of passive policy is the pricing experience of the airlines. Although safety considerations and differences in equipment and service cloud the picture, it is pretty clear that the bargain-rate coach fares of scheduled airlines were adopted in reaction to the cut rates of nonscheduled airlines. This competitive response has apparently established a new pattern of traffic growth for the scheduled airlines.

An example of penetration pricing at the initial stage of the product's market life—again from the book field—occurred when Simon & Schuster adopted the policy of bringing out new titles in a low-priced, paper-bound edition simultaneously with the conventional higher-priced, cloth-bound edition.

What conditions warrant aggressive pricing for market penetration? This question cannot be answered categorically, but it may be helpful to generalize that the following conditions indicate the desirability of an early low-price policy:

- A high price-elasticity of demand in the short run, i.e., a high degree of responsiveness of sales to reductions in price.

- Substantial savings in production costs as the result of greater volume—not a necessary condition, however, since if elasticity of demand is high enough, pricing for market expansion may be profitable without realizing production economies.

- Product characteristics such that it will not seem bizarre when it is first fitted into the consumers' expenditure pattern.

- A strong threat of potential competition.

This threat of potential competition is a highly persuasive reason for penetration pricing. One of the major objectives of most low-pricing policies in the pioneering stages of market development is to raise entry barriers to prospective competitors. This is appropriate when entrants must make large-scale investments to reach minimum costs and they cannot slip into an established market by selling at substantial discounts.

In many industries, however, the important potential competitor is a large, multiple-product firm operating as well in other fields than that represented by the product in question. For a firm, the most important consideration for entry is not existing margins but the prospect of large and growing volume of sales. Present margins over costs are not the dominant consideration because such firms are normally confident that they can get their costs down as low as competitors' costs if the volume of production is large.

Therefore, when total industry sales are not expected to amount to much, a high-margin policy can be followed because entry is improbable in view of the expectation of low volume and because it does not matter too much to potential competitors if the new product is introduced.

The fact remains that for products whose market potential appears big, a policy of stayout pricing from the outset makes much more sense. When a leading soap manufacturer developed an additive that whitened clothes and enhanced the brilliance of colors, the company chose to take its gains in a larger share of the market rather than in a temporary price premium. Such a decision was sound, since the company's competitors could be expected to match or better the product improvement fairly promptly. Under these circumstances, the price premium would have been short-lived, whereas the gains in market share were more likely to be retained.

Of course, any decision to start out with lower prices must take into account the fact that if the new product calls for capital recovery over a long period, the risk may be great that later entrants will be able to exploit new production techniques which can undercut the pioneer's original cost structure. In such cases, the low-price pattern should be adopted with a view to long-run rather than to short-run profits, with recognition that it usually takes time to attain the volume potentialities of the market.

It is sound to calculate profits in dollar terms rather than in percentage margins, and to think in terms of percentage return on the investment required to produce and sell the expanded volume rather than in terms of percentage markup. Profit calculation should also recognize the contributions that market-development pricing can make to the sale of other products and to the long-run future of the company. Often a decision to use development pricing will turn on these considerations of long-term impacts upon the firm's total operation strategy rather than on the profits directly attributable to the individual product.

An example of market-expansion pricing is found in the experience of a producer of asbestos shingles, which had a limited sale in the high-price house market. The company wanted to broaden the market in order to

compete effectively with other roofing products for the
inexpensive home. It tried to find the price of asphalt
shingles that would make the annual cost per unit of roof
over a period of years as low as the cheaper roofing that
was currently commanding the mass market. Indications
were that the price would have to be at least this low
before volume sales would come.

Next, the company explored the relationship between
production costs and volume, far beyond the range of its
own volume experience. Variable costs and overhead
costs were estimated separately, and the possibilities of a
different organization of production were explored. Calculating in terms of anticipated dollars of profit rather
than in terms of percentage margin, the company
reduced the price of asbestos shingles and brought the
annual cost down close to the cost of the cheapest
asphalt roof. This reduction produced a greatly
expanded volume and secured a substantial share of the
mass market.

Pricing in Maturity

To determine what pricing policies are appropriate for
later stages in the cycle of market and competitive maturity, the manufacturer must be able to tell when a product is approaching maturity. Some of the symptoms of
degeneration of competitive status toward the commodity level are:

- **Weakening in brand preference.** This may be evi-
  denced by a higher cross-elasticity of demand among
  leading products, the leading brand not being able to
  continue demanding as much price premium as initially without losing position.

- **Narrowing physical variation among products as the best designs are developed and standardized.** This has been dramatically demonstrated in automobiles and is still in process in television receivers.

- **The entry in force of private-label competitors.** This is exemplified by the mail-order houses' sale of own-label refrigerators and paint sprayers.

- **Market saturation.** The ratio of replacement sales to new equipment sales serves as an indicator of the competitive degeneration of durable goods, but in general it must be kept in mind that both market size and degree of saturation are hard to define (e.g., saturation of the radio market, which was initially thought to be one radio per home and later had to be expanded to one radio per room).

- **The stabilization of production methods.** A dramatic innovation that slashes costs (e.g., prefabricated houses) may disrupt what appears to be a well-stabilized oligopoly market.

The first step for the manufacturer whose specialty is about to slip into the commodity category is to reduce real prices promptly as soon as symptoms of deterioration appear. This step is essential if the manufacturer is to forestall the entry of private-label competitors. Examples of failure to make such a reduction are abundant.

By and large, private-label competition has speeded up the inevitable evolution of high specialities into commodities and has tended to force margins down by making price reductions more open and more universal than they would otherwise be. From one standpoint, the rapid growth of the private-label share in the market is a symptom of unwise pricing on the part of the national-brand sector of the industry.

This does not mean that manufacturers should declare open price war in the industry. When they move into mature competitive stages they enter oligopoly relationships where price slashing is peculiarly dangerous and unpopular. But, with active competition in prices precluded, competitive efforts may move in other directions, particularly toward product improvement and market segmentation.

Product improvement at this stage, where most of the important developments have been put into all brands, practically amounts to market segmentation. For it means adding refinements and quality extras that put the brand in the elite category, with an appeal only to the top-income brackets. This is a common tactic in food marketing, and in the tire industry it was the response of the General Tire Company to the competitive conditions of the 1930s.

As the product matures and as its distinctiveness narrows, a choice must sometimes be made by the company concerning the rung of the competitive price ladder it should occupy—roughly, the choice between a low and a not-so-low relative price.

A price at the low end of the array of the industry's real prices is usually associated with a product mixture showing a lean element of services and reputation (the product being physically similar to competitive brands, however) and a company having a lower gross margin than the other industry members (although not necessarily a lower net margin). The choice of such a low-price policy may be dictated by technical or market inferiorities of the product, or it may be adopted because the company has faith in the long-run price elasticity of demand and the ability of low prices to penetrate an important segment of the market not tapped by higher prices. The classic example is Henry Ford's pricing decision in the 1920s.

In Summary

In pricing products of perishable distinctiveness, a company must study the cycle of competitive degeneration in order to determine its major causes, its probable speed, and the chances of slowing it down. Pricing in the pioneering stage of the cycle involves difficult problems of projecting potential demand and of guessing the relation of price to sales.

The first step in this process is to explore consumer preferences and to establish the feasibility of the product, in order to get a rough idea of whether demand will warrant further exploration. The second step is to mark out a range of prices that will make the product economically attractive to buyers. The third step is to estimate the probable sales that will result from alternative prices.

If these initial explorations are encouraging, the next move is to make decisions on promotional strategy and distribution channels. The policy of relatively high prices in the pioneering stage has much to commend it, particularly when sales seem to be comparatively unresponsive to price but quite responsive to educational promotion.

On the other hand, the policy of relatively low prices in the pioneering stage, in anticipation of the cost savings resulting from an expanding market, has been strikingly successful under the right conditions. Low prices look to long-run rather than short-run profits and discourage potential competitors.

Pricing in the mature stages of a product's life cycle requires a technique for recognizing when a product is approaching maturity. Pricing problems in this stage border closely on those of oligopoly.

Retrospective Commentary

Twenty-five years have brought important changes and have taught us much, but the basics of pricing pioneer products are the same, only clearer. New product pricing, if the product is truly novel, is in essence monopoly pricing—modified only because the monopoly power of the new product is (1) restricted because buyers have alternatives, (2) ephemeral because it is subject to inevitable erosion as competitors equal or better it, and (3) controllable because actions of the seller can affect the amount and the durability of the new product's market power.

In pricing, the buyers' viewpoint should be controlling. For example, buyer's-rate-of-return pricing of new capital equipment looks at your price through the eyes of the customer. It recognizes that the upper limit is the price that will produce the minimum acceptable rate of return on the investment of a sufficiently large number of prospects. This return has a broad range for two reasons. First, the added profits obtainable from the use of your equipment will differ among customers and among applications for the same customer. Second, prospective customers also differ in the minimum rate of return that will induce them to invest in your product.

This capital-budgeting approach opens a new kind of demand analysis, which involves inquiry into: (1) the costs of buyers from displaceable alternative ways of doing the job, (2) the cost-saving and profit-producing capability of your equipment, and (3) the capital management policies of your customers, particularly their cost of capital and cutoff criteria.

ROLE OF COST

Cost should play a role in new product pricing quite different from that in traditional cost-plus pricing. To use cost wisely requires answers to some questions of theory: Whose cost? Which cost? What role?

As to whose cost, three persons are important: prospective buyers, existent and potential competitors, and the producer of the new product. For each of the three, cost should play a different role, and the concept of cost should differ accordingly.

The role of prospective *buyers'* costs is to forecast their response to alternative prices by determining what your product will do to the costs of your buyers. Rate-of-return pricing of capital goods illustrates this buyer's-cost approach, which is applicable in principle to all new products.

Cost is usually the crucial estimate in appraising *competitors'* capabilities. Two kinds of competitor costs need to be forecasted. The first is for products already in the marketplace. One purpose is to predict staying power; for this the cost concept is competitors' long-run incremental cost. Another purpose may be to guess the floor of retaliation pricing; for this we need competitors' short-run incremental cost.

The second kind is the cost of a competitive product that is unborn but that could eventually displace yours. Time-spotted prediction of the performance characteristics, the costs, and the probable prices of future new products is both essential and possible. Such a prediction is essential because it determines the economic life expectancy of your product and the shape of its competitiveness cycle.

This prediction is possible, first, because the pace of technical advance in product design is persistent and can usually be determined by statistical study of past progress. It is possible, second, because the rate at which competitors' cost will slide down the cost compression curve that results from cost-saving investments in manufacturing equipment, methods, and worker learning is usually a logarithmic function of cumulative output. Thus this rate can be ascertained and projected.

The *producer's* cost should play several different roles in pricing a new product, depending on the decision involved. The first decision concerns capital control. A new product must be priced before any significant investment is made in research and must be periodically repriced when more money is invested as its development progresses toward market. The concept of cost that is relevant for this decision is the predicted full cost, which should include imputed cost of capital on intangible investment over the whole life cycle of the new product. Its profitability and investment return are meaningless for any shorter period.

A second decision is "birth control." The commercialization decision calls for a similar concept of cost and discounted cash-flow investment analysis, but one that is confined to incremental investment beyond product birth.

Another role of cost is to establish a price floor that is also the threshold for selecting from candidate prices those that will maximize return on a new product investment at different stages of its life. The relevant concept here is future short-run incremental cost.

SEGMENTATION PRICING

Particularly for new products, an important tactic is differential pricing for separated market segments. To enhance profits, we split the market into sectors that differ in price sensitivity, charging higher prices to those who are impervious and lower prices to the more sensitive souls.

One requisite is the ability to identify and seal off groups of prospects who differ in sensitivity of sales to price or differ in the effectiveness of competition (cross-elasticity of demand). Another is that leakage from the low price segment must be small and costs of segregation low enough to make it worthwhile.

One device is time segmentation: a skimming price strategy at the outset followed by penetration pricing as the product matures. Another device is price-shaped modification of a basic product to enhance traits for which one group of customers will pay dearly (e.g., reliability for the military).

A similar device is product-configuration differentials (notably extras: the roof of the Stanley Steamer was an extra when it was a new product). Another is afterlife pricing (e.g., repair parts, expendable components, and auxiliary services). Also, trade channel discounts commonly achieve profitable price discrimination (as with original equipment discounts).

COST COMPRESSION CURVE

Cost forecasting for pricing new products should be based on the cost compression curve, which relates real manufacturing cost per unit of value added to the cumulative quantity produced. This cost function (sometimes labeled "learning curve" or "experience curve") is mainly the consequence of cost cutting investments (largely intangible) to discover and achieve internal substitutions, automation, worker learning, scale economies, and technological advances. Usually these move together as a logarithmic function of accumulated output.

Cost compression curve pricing of technically advanced products (for example, a microprocessor) epitomizes penetration pricing. It condenses the time span of the process of cutting prices *ahead* of forecasted cost savings in order to beat competitors to the bigger market and the resulting manufacturing economies that are opened up because of creative pricing.

This cost compression curve pricing strategy, which took two decades for the Model T's life span, is condensed into a few months for the integrated circuit. But though the speed and the sources of saving are different, the principle is the same: a steep cost compression curve suggests penetration pricing of a new product. Such pricing is most attractive when the product superiority over rivals is small and ephemeral and when entry and expansion by competitors is easy and probable.

IMPACTS OF INFLATION

Continuous high-speed inflation has important impacts on new product pricing. It changes the goal. It renders obsolete accounted earnings per share as the corporation's overriding goal—replacing it with maximization of the present worth (discounted at the corporation's cost of capital) of the future stream of real purchasing power dividends (including a terminal dividend or capital gain). Real earnings in terms of cash-flow buying power alone determine the power to pay real dividends.

Inflation raises the buyers' benchmark costs of the new products' competitive alternatives. Thus it lifts the

buyer benefits obtainable from the new products' protected distinctiveness (for example, it saves more wage
dollars).

It raises the seller's required return on the investment
to create and to launch the new product. Why? Because
the cost of equity capital and of debt capital will be made
higher to compensate for anticipated inflation. For the
same reason, inflation raises the customer's cutoff point
of minimum acceptable return. It also intensifies the
rivalry for scarce investment dollars among the seller's
new product candidates. Hence it probably tends to
increase stillbirths, but may lower subsequent infant
mortality. For these reasons, perennial inflation will
make an economic attack on the problem of pricing new
products even more compelling.

Pricing of new products remains an art. But the experienced judgment required to price and reprice the product over its life cycle to fit its changing competitive environment may be improved by considering seven pricing
precepts suggested by this analysis.

1. Pricing a new product is an occasion for rethinking
   the overriding corporate goal. This goal should be to
   maximize the present worth, discounted at the corporation's cost of capital, of the future stream of real
   (purchasing-power) dividends, including a terminal
   dividend or capital gain. The Wall Street traditional
   objective—maximizing the size or the growth of
   book earnings per share—is an inferior master goal
   that is made obsolete by inflation.

2. The unit for making decisions and for measuring
   return on investment is the entire economic life of
   the new product. Reported annual profits on a new
   product have little economic significance. The pricing implications of the new product's changing

competitive status as it passes through its life cycle from birth to obsolescence are intricate but compelling.

3. Pricing of a new product should begin long before its birth, and repricing should continue over its life cycle. Prospective prices coupled with forecasted costs should control the decision to invest in its development, the determination to launch it commercially, and the decision to kill it.

4. A new product should be viewed through the eyes of the buyer. Rate of return on customers' investment should be the main consideration in pricing a pioneering capital good: the buyers' savings (and added earnings), expressed as return on their investment in the new product, are the key to both estimating price sensitivity of demand and pricing profitably.

5. Costs can supply useful guidance in new product pricing, but not by the conventional wisdom of cost-plus pricing. Costs of three persons are pertinent: the buyer, the competitor, and the producer. The role of cost differs among the three, as does the concept of cost that is pertinent to that role: different costs for different decisions.

6. A strategy of price skimming can be distinguished from a strategy of penetration pricing. Skimming is appropriate at the outset for some pioneering products, particularly when followed by penetration pricing (for example, the price cascade of a new book). In contrast, a policy of penetration pricing from the outset, in anticipation of the cost compression curve for manufacturing costs, is usually best when this curve falls steeply and projectably, and is buttressed

by economies of scale and of advancing technology, and when demand is price sensitive and invasion is threatened.

7. Penetration and skimming pricing can be used at the same time in different sectors of the market. Creating opportunities to split the market into segments that differ in price sensitivity and in competitiveness, so as to simultaneously charge higher prices in insensitive segments and price low to elastic sectors, can produce extra profits and faster cost-compression for a new product. Devices are legion.

Originally published in November 1950
Reprint 76604

Six Sigma Pricing

MANMOHAN S. SODHI AND

NAVDEEP S. SODHI

Executive Summary

MANY COMPANIES ARE now good at managing costs
and wringing out manufacturing efficiencies. The TQM
movement and the disciplines of Six Sigma have seen to
that. But the discipline so often brought to the cost side of
the business equation is found far less commonly on the
revenue side.

The authors describe how a global manufacturer of
industrial equipment, which they call Acme Incorporated,
recently applied Six Sigma to one major revenue-related
activity—the price-setting process. It seemed to Acme's
executives that pricing closely resembled many manufacturing processes. So, with the help of a Six Sigma black
belt from manufacturing, a manager from Acme's pricing
division recruited a team to carry out the five Six Sigma
steps:

- **Define what constitutes a defect.** At Acme, a defect was an item sold at an unauthorized price.

- **Gather data and prepare it for analysis.** That involved mapping out the existing pricing-agreement process.

- **Analyze the data.** The team identified the ways in which people failed to carry out or assert effective control at each stage.

- **Recommended modifications to the existing process.** The team sought to decrease the number of unapproved prices without creating an onerous approval apparatus.

- **Create controls.** This step enabled Acme to sustain and extend the improvements in its pricing procedures.

As a result of the changes, Acme earned $6 million in additional revenue on one product line alone in the six months following implementation—money that went straight to the bottom line. At the same time, the company removed much of the organizational friction that had long bedeviled its pricing process. Other companies can benefit from Acme's experience as they look for ways to exercise price control without alienating customers.

M ANY COMPANIES HAVE become good at managing costs and mastering manufacturing efficiencies. The TQM and Six Sigma movements have seen to that. But the discipline so often brought to the cost side of the business equation is far less common on the revenue side. As a result, many companies continue to leak cash from the top line.

In this article, we describe how a global manufacturer of industrial equipment, which we will call Acme Incorporated, applied Six Sigma rigor to its price-setting process for one product line to great effect. Acme met its target of increasing annual revenue by $500,000 in less than three months. When Acme subsequently raised list prices across the board, the company reaped the full value of the increase for this product line, but much less in others. And in just six months, annual revenue increases reached an eye-popping $5.8 million for this product line alone, all of which went straight to the bottom line as well.

Not only did the reforms stem the revenue leaks, they also removed much of the organizational friction that had long bedeviled the company's pricing process by making it clear who had authority over which pricing decisions. Uncertainty about pricing policy (or rather the appearance of it) may help salespeople in their negotiations with customers, but it does a company no good for its own people to be confused and conflicted on that score.

At Acme, that tension was readily apparent. On the one hand, Acme's sales reps saw their mission as building market share—senior management's stated aim. Being close to the customer, they felt they knew what the best price was. They saw the pricing managers and analysts as an obstruction, out of touch and too slow to respond to changing facts on the ground. They would often circumvent the necessary checks and controls on invoiced prices, potentially eroding the company's profit margins.

For their part, the pricing analysts saw themselves as the guardians of Acme's profitability, providing essential pricing analysis and, in their opinion, quick turnaround on approvals. As we will see, the Six Sigma project generated hard evidence that significantly reduced the tension in this uneasy Sales–Pricing relationship, which became less influenced by gut instinct or emotion.

The Problem

The trigger for the project was a change in market conditions, which put Acme under considerable pricing pressure. The price of two key raw materials, steel and petroleum, had risen quickly and sharply, threatening to inflict a projected $20 million in unplanned annual incremental costs on the company. Some of its steel suppliers had even refused to honor existing contracts. Overall, average costs had doubled within the space of a few months.

The company had no choice but to raise list prices. But by how much? Raise prices too much, and Acme stood to lose customers to rivals. Raise prices too little, and it would not be worth the effort to announce and implement the change. Moreover, Acme could not be sure whether a nominal increase in list prices would even hit the bottom line. The organization's pricing processes made it difficult to control the price that was actually invoiced.

Acme's myriad products could each be configured in numerous ways, according to customers' needs, and the company published list prices for every possible configuration. But each sale then had its own individually approved discount and hence its own invoiced price. Prices and discounts were set by the pricing division. Acme's sales division had market-specific blanket ceilings for percentage discounts on all products, and sales reps had to obtain authorization from Pricing to offer deeper discounts. Pricing either approved the request or set a slightly higher approved price, typically expressed as a percentage of the list price. After the transaction was completed, Sales invoiced the customer with a final transaction price, which was (in principle) the same as or slightly higher than the approved price.

But it was well known that top management frowned on losing market share, and the absence of any effective controls encouraged some salespeople to short-circuit the process. A sales representative would ask Pricing for a discount that was much deeper than the guidelines allowed for, and even if Pricing complied, the representative might offer a further, unapproved discount to close a deal. For instance, one order approved by Pricing at $81,000 was actually invoiced at $75,000, and another at $31,000 was invoiced at $28,000.

With tens of thousands of sales transactions per year, the task of making sure each invoice accorded with the list and approved prices was daunting. But the lack of control over final prices meant that even if Acme could work out how much of a hike in list prices the market could bear, the company still could not be sure it would actually see the increase in each transaction or even overall, across transactions.

The Project

How to get a grip on the situation? Senior managers began by considering what other parts of the organization had done to bring similarly variable processes under control. They knew that Acme had enjoyed considerable success in reducing manufacturing variability by applying the famous Six Sigma discipline. Employees from different functions and organizational levels understood the methodology, and some had company-specific Six Sigma certification, holding titles like Green Belt and Black Belt, following the example of such companies as Motorola and General Electric.

It seemed to Acme's executives that pricing closely resembled many manufacturing processes. A product's invoiced price could be considered a final product, the result of a "manufacturing" process encompassing several stages. They decided, therefore, to pilot a Six Sigma pricing project in one of the company's North American subsidiaries. If the project led to better control of final prices, they could roll out the approach throughout the company's entire global operations.

A manager from Pricing was appointed as project manager to carry out the five Six Sigma steps: define, measure, analyze, improve, and control. He was given the help of a Six Sigma expert, or Master Black Belt, recruited from the manufacturing side. The project sponsor was the senior executive responsible for pricing.

DEFINITION

The first step in any Six Sigma project is to clarify the problem and narrow its scope in such a way that measurable goals can be achieved within a few months. Then a team is assembled to examine the process in detail, suggest improvements, and implement those recommendations. In the manufacturing realm, project managers and their sponsors typically begin by defining what constitutes a defect and then establish a set of objectives designed to reduce the occurrence of such defects. (The phrase "Six Sigma" in fact implies a goal of reducing the number of defects to less than 3.4 per million occurrences, assuming that the quality of a product's attributes varies according to a normal bell-shaped distribution pattern.)

Acme's project manager proposed that a defect should be defined as a transaction invoiced at a price lower than the one Pricing had approved (or lower than those allowed by the current blanket guidelines, when approval had not been sought). Note that defects are being defined in relative terms, according to the blanket discount ceilings set for the salespeople and the guidelines established by the pricing analysts. If the market were to take a turn for the worse, the ceilings could be raised; if the market were to strengthen, they could be lowered. A defect occurs only when the actual invoiced price is out of compliance with the guidelines.

Once the definition of a defect was set, the project manager, with the help of the sponsor, recommended an appropriate scope for the project—that is, whether it should be limited to only one particular product line or applied to several. In this case, the project sponsor limited the scope to a single product line.

The next step for the project manager is to propose a charter for the project that specifies the expected deliverables. Given the definition of a defective price, it was clear that this project would have to deliver:

- a better understanding of the existing pricing process;

- a modified process to control and, hence, improve final transaction prices;

- ways to track improvement in final prices and to monitor compliance with the process and with pricing guidelines.

Next, to collect data, carry out analysis, and ensure everyone's buy-in for any subsequent implementation, the project manager enlisted people from the pricing, finance, marketing, IT, and sales divisions to be part of the Six Sigma team. The various team members were selected for their functional and analytical expertise. The finance person, for example, was chosen because she was familiar with the many pricing-related reports Acme was currently generating and also with many of the company's data sources.

In addition, to endow the project with institutional backing and to ensure that team members had good access to data, the project manager asked people in positions of influence at Acme to serve on a steering committee for the project. The chair of the committee was the project sponsor. Other members included the director of sales, the vice president of IT, the vice president of finance, and the vice president of marketing. They agreed that the project manager would meet with the team and the steering committee as needed to keep them apprised of the project's progress.

The first duty of the team was to confirm the proposed problem definition and project charter and to set a financial goal for the project. That was no easy task, as it was the first time Acme had embarked on such a project. Nonetheless, the team set a goal of increasing revenues by $500,000 in the first year following implementation. This additional revenue was to come entirely from more efficient price management—in other words, from actions that did not incur any losses in market share or sales volumes. This was a far more ambitious number than Acme had ever set for comparable manufacturing or service Six Sigma projects, which had typically delivered average annual cost savings of less than $100,000.

MEASUREMENT

In the second step of a Six Sigma project, the team gathers data and prepares it for analysis. At Acme, the project manager began by mapping the price agreement process, with team members helping to fill in process details. To generate and verify the information he needed, the project manager formally interviewed eight colleagues from five functional divisions: IT, sales, pricing, finance, and marketing. He also sought informal feedback from other people in these functions. As a result of this exercise, the team was able to draw a high-level diagram of the entire process showing the flow of information from one step to the next (see the exhibit "What Are We Doing?").

The map was supported by documentation detailing the inputs (called X's, in Six Sigma parlance) and outputs (Y's) associated with each step, showing all the people and IT systems involved, and specifying whether the decision-making inputs could be controlled by Pricing or Sales. The eventual output variable for the entire process is the final transaction price, but intermediate steps have their own intermediate outputs. For example, after an initial discussion with a customer, the output could be an agreed upon price that conforms to guidelines, or it might be a proposed price that would have to be referred to Pricing for approval. The inputs are the characteristics of the deal, such as the product type, order size, or time of year.

The map revealed a pricing process with six main steps, which seemed straightforward in principle. But it was clear that in practice the sequence did not work smoothly, that it was replete with exceptions and short-cuts, and that the quality of inputs available to Sales or Pricing personnel in any step could be quite poor.

What Are We Doing?

When Acme's Six Sigma team mapped the company's existing pricing process, it became easy to see not only how the process was supposed to work but how it actually worked. The formal process comprised six main steps, which should have been taken in sequence (as depicted with solid lines). But oftentimes, sales reps sidestepped it all by negotiating final prices with the customer directly. Other times, the process got bogged down as pricing analysts rooted around for information they should have already obtained from the sales staff in Step 2 or negotiations went back and forth between the sales rep and the pricing analyst (essentially getting stuck before Step 6).

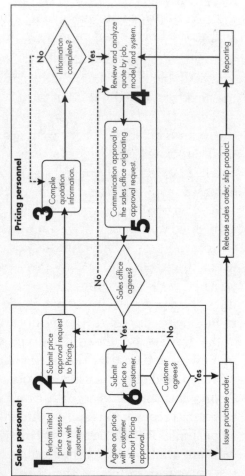

1. **Perform initial price assessment with customer (Sales).** The inputs for this are the list price, the blanket discount guidelines for Sales in the particular market, and the customer's product and pricing requirements. The output is a tentative price (that is, a discount off the list price). Approval is needed from Pricing if the discount is deeper than the maximum authorized for the particular market.

2. **Submit price approval request to Pricing (Sales).** For the Pricing personnel receiving such a request, the inputs are the price the sales rep has requested and the guidelines for pricing analysts. In practice, sometimes this step, and most of the subsequent ones, were circumvented when a sales rep offered a final discounted price to the customer without prior Pricing approval.

3. **Compile quotation information (Pricing).** The input is the information about the customer and the order provided by the sales rep to support his or her request. The output is the complete details of the transaction in question. This step should be trivial but often, in practice, the sales rep did not or could not provide enough information about the quotation, and the Pricing analyst or manager would have to chase around to get the missing information.

4. **Review and analyze quote (Pricing).** Inputs are the completed quotation information generated in the previous steps (including the tentative price the sales rep has requested); reports summarizing the history of similar transactions in the particular market; and, when available, reports of similar transactions with the same customer. In theory, such reports would

guide Pricing's efforts to accept or modify the price requested and to produce the output—the tentative approved price. In reality, with information scattered in different computer systems, the guidelines available to the pricing analyst could be quite poor. Or the sales rep might request a very quick turnaround, leaving little time for a pricing analyst to carry out this step effectively.

5. **Communicate approval to sales office (Pricing).** The input is the tentative approved price from the analysis in the previous step and any additional information regarding the order and customer. The output is the approved price. This should be the penultimate step before the sales rep approaches the customer but, in practice, this could instead be the beginning of a prolonged negotiation between Sales and Pricing. Other people may weigh in at this point as well, and the final approved price could end up quite a bit lower because of pressure from a manager or from a more senior sales or marketing executive.

6. **Submit price to customer (Sales).** The input is the approved price. The output is the tentative price for invoicing that the sales rep submits to the customer. At this point, the sales rep should simply be offering the customer the approved price. But this entire project was based on the observation that the price the sales rep actually offered the customer, as indicated by the invoice from the subsequent transaction (if there was one), could be quite a bit lower than the approved price.

Before moving on to the next stage of the project, the team assessed the quality of the input data that supported the pricing process. It would be difficult to improve the process if the current steps systematically produced faulty data. Moreover, the team needed to have faith in the numbers on which it was going to base its findings and recommendations. By examining representative samples of data in detail, the team was able to confirm that the actual sales transaction data were by and large stable and reliable, even though different reports presented the information in different formats.

ANALYSIS

Once a process has been mapped and documented, and the quality of the hard data supporting it has been verified, the Six Sigma team can begin the analysis. The team members usually start by meeting to identify the ways in which people fail to act as needed or fail to assert effective control at each stage.

To aid in this analysis, the Acme team used a common Six Sigma tool called the Cause and Effect (C&E) Matrix to guide discussion. With the help of the Master Black Belt, the project manager held a workshop using the tool to identify problems and put them in order of priority. The rows on the C&E matrix list all the steps in the current process, and the columns list all of the requirements a particular process customer has for the entire process. Each requirement is then weighted according to how important it is to that customer. (See the exhibit "Which Steps Matter?") For Acme's team, the customers were senior executives who wanted better controls in the pricing process and, eventually, better price performance.

The team did not actually assign number scores. Instead, members used the structure of the matrix to

Which Steps Matter?

The Cause and Effect Matrix is one of the basic tools of any Six Sigma project. It is a systematic way to judge the impact of each step on the process's customers (whether internal or external) as a prelude to prioritizing underlying problems and identifying their causes. In this example, we've filled in two steps, and senior management is the customer.

1. List the customer's requirements for the process as a whole.

2. Rate how important each requirement is to the customer.

3. Describe each step in the process.

4. List all of its inputs.

5. Rate the effect each step has on the customer requirement.

6. Multiply the importance rating by the effect score for each step. Add across to get a score that indicates how important the step is for meeting the customer's requirements.

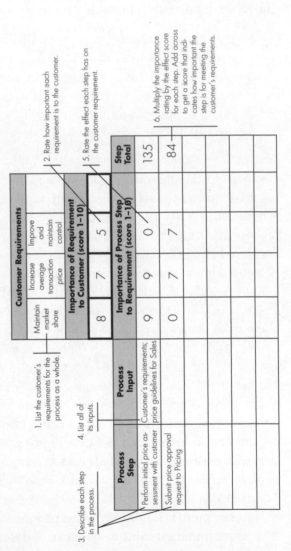

		Customer Requirements			
		Maintain market share	Increase average transaction price	Improve and maintain control	
		Importance of Requirement to Customer (score 1–10)			
		8	7	5	
Process Step	Process Input	Importance of Process Step to Requirement (score 1–10)			Step Total
Perform initial price assessment with customer	Customer's requirements; price guidelines for Sales	9	9	0	135
Submit price approval request to Pricing		0	7	7	84

focus on possible causes for lack of control at each step. The process diagram was projected as a slide, and team members used a whiteboard to discuss each step in turn. The main findings from this exercise suggested that the defects arose largely from problems in steps 1, 4, and 6, and from failures in reporting.

- **Step 1.** The team found that the ability of the sales reps to help customers select the right products, and the right features for those products, was critical to managing customers' price expectations. Unfortunately, salespeople's failures in assessing customer requirements could not be easily detected and controlled.

- **Step 4.** The key constraint here was time; sales reps sometimes wanted discount approval within hours of forwarding a request, which made it difficult for pricing analysts to work out whether or not the discount was reasonable. Giving Pricing more time for analysis would make it easier to reduce the incidence of defective prices.

- **Step 6.** Sales reps sometimes offered final prices to customers without prior approval, leaving Pricing with little choice but to OK the price after the fact. The team agreed that such situations should be tracked.

- **Reporting.** Information about transactions was not gathered or presented in a consistent manner. The unit's various functions generated more than a hundred different transaction reports that summarized sales data by product line, market, and other ways at weekly, monthly, or quarterly intervals. Discrepancies and redundancies in those reports led to variability in the decisions analysts came to in deciding prices. This meant that managers could neither track pricing defects easily nor obtain the data they needed for Step 4 in time to do adequate due diligence on price quotes.

After completing the C&E workshop, the project manager did a standard statistical analysis of transaction-level data for all of the individual transactions that occurred in the two years before the project started. As the exhibit "What Are We Really Charging?" reveals, he confirmed that actual transaction prices were distributed

---

What Are We Really Charging?

At Acme, analysis of two years' sales data showed that the higher the list price, the deeper the mean discount tended to be. For large transactions with list prices in the $200,000 range, for instance, the mean price nego-tiated with the customer was in the $5,000 range, the mean price Acme actually charged was 60% of the list price. This suggested that Acme could improve average prices by differentiating the pricing guidelines for transactions of different sizes—precluding deep discounts, for instance, on small transactions.

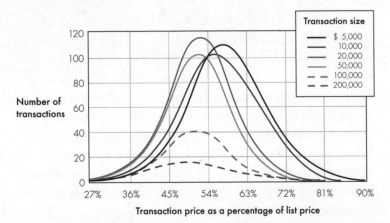

Transaction price as a percentage of list price

along normal bell-shaped curves around the average transaction prices. But he also discovered distinct bell curves for different transaction sizes: average discounts increased the higher the list price of the transaction. That indicated that many customers were willing to pay higher prices for smaller transactions, suggesting that pricing guidelines could and should be differentiated for different-sized transactions.

In addition, the analysis revealed that salespeople serving certain territories within the same market had a greater tendency than their colleagues in other territories to invoice at prices either significantly higher or lower than approved. The team concluded from this analysis that different pricing guidelines needed to be set not only for different transaction sizes but also for different territories within the same market and possibly even for different customer groups. Pricing guidelines had always been market specific but were not differentiated by transaction size, by territory, or, for the most part, by customer group.

IMPROVEMENT

The results from the analysis created a lot of positive buzz among Acme's senior managers. It was time to recommend modifications to the existing process to decrease the number of unapproved prices without creating an onerous approval process. Response speed was critical for salespeople so they could continue to act quickly and close deals. But this was a challenge for pricing personnel. What they needed, the team concluded, was clear guidelines to help them decide when they should or should not approve any deeper-than-usual discounts that Sales had requested or promised to customers.

So the team proposed giving graduated discount approval authority to individuals in three levels of the organization's hierarchy: sales reps or managers, pricing analysts, and the pricing manager. Finally, at a fourth level, top executives could continue to approve discounts without any limit. So, for example, in one particular market for a transaction size between $100,000 and $150,000, a sales representative could offer any discount up to 30%, but to be able to offer an even lower price to a customer, he would have to contact a pricing analyst for approval. She would first check against the guideline price for that region, type of product, transaction size, and perhaps other criteria, and use this to negotiate with the sales rep any further discount, up to 35%. If the sales rep felt that the situation demanded an even lower price than the analyst could authorize, the request would be elevated to the pricing manager, who could approve a discount of up to 40%. If the salesperson was going for an even lower price, the request was passed up to a specified group at the top leadership level, which alone could approve a higher discount. Making both the guidelines and the escalation process clear made the process more efficient and faster.

In cases where sales representatives had already offered a customer a price and needed post hoc authorization, the new process required that the rep involve his boss, who would have to e-mail or call Pricing for approval. The price already offered would still be honored, but now reps could be held more accountable for making unauthorized commitments.

The new distribution of pricing responsibilities required a process for developing—and, from time to time, reevaluating—all of the discount limits. To ensure that limits did not become outdated, the team created a spreadsheet tool that let Pricing work off recent transaction history.

The team also created exception codes that enabled Acme to track the reasons for variations in prices. The codes made it clear who had been involved in the decision to deviate from guidelines. For instance, if someone from the leadership had approved a deep discount, the eventual transaction was tagged with a Leadership Approval code. If Acme needed to match a competitor's aggressive price, the pricing manager could approve a low price that was tagged with a Competitive Match code. If a sales rep had already promised a price to a customer before getting approval, the transaction would have to be tagged with a Sales Error code. What's more, Pricing would now have 24 hours to do due diligence before approving a price request, and Acme tracked which sales reps consistently asked for extra-fast turnarounds.

CONTROL

In the final stage of a Six Sigma project, the team creates controls that enable the company to sustain and extend the improvements. Acme set up a monthly review at which executives—mainly the vice presidents of marketing, sales, and finance, along with their direct reports— look at the company's overall performance and at particular geographic markets and transaction sizes to see if the new process is indeed resulting in higher average transaction prices, fewer exceptions, and no loss in market share. If prices are under control but the company is losing market share, it might be a sign that Acme needs to review its pricing guidelines or the way sales reps are managing their territories. If the review group notices that a particular sales rep is frequently making Sales Error transactions, the rep's boss will take a closer look at how that person is negotiating. And if the review group sees that transactions of a particular size regularly require the pricing manager's approval, the group would instigate a reexamination of the pricing guidelines for that transaction size.

The Payoff

The initial goal of generating half a million dollars in incremental revenues in the first year was handily exceeded in only three months. More important, following a subsequent across-the-board list price increase, the average transaction price for the pilot product line went up by slightly more than the list prices; in other words, the increase was fully reflected in the top line. But other product lines realized less than half the increase. That list price increase, together with the tighter controls the Six Sigma team developed and implemented, resulted in the $5.8 million in incremental sales in just the first six months following implementation going straight to the bottom line.

From an organizational perspective, the Six Sigma approach has considerably reduced the friction inherent in the Pricing–Sales relationship. The exercise of systematically collecting and analyzing price transaction data gave pricing analysts hard evidence to counter the more intuitive claims that the sales staff had typically advanced in negotiating discounts. A frequent refrain, for instance, was: "My customers want just as high a percentage discount for a $3,000 transaction as they would get for a $300,000 one." Now that Pricing knows for certain that Acme's customers tend to accept lower discounts on smaller transactions and that some customers are willing to pay higher prices than others, analysts can more easily push back when negotiating price approvals with sales staff. They can respond confidently and authoritatively when sales reps ask questions like "Why is my authorized price higher than those in another market?" or "How come we don't authorize the same price for all customers?"

Salespeople, for their part, are less likely to feel that the negotiation with Pricing is driven by political motives or by a purely personal desire to assert control, and they can, of course, use the same data to press their own points. It became clear, for example, that some sales offices that had previously been under scrutiny for aggressive pricing practices had in fact been acting perfectly reasonably given their local market conditions.

In light of the project's success and its low cost, Acme is rolling out Six Sigma pricing across the entire organization. Other companies operating in competitive environments can also benefit from Acme's experience as they look for ways to exercise price control without alienating customers. They can transform the tenor of the relationship between their pricing and sales staffs from adversity to relative harmony by giving them a process for making joint decisions that are aligned with company objectives and based on solid data and analysis.

Originally published in May 2005
Reprint R0505H

Price Smarter on the Net

WALTER BAKER, MICHAEL V. MARN, AND
CRAIG ZAWADA

Executive Summary

COMPANIES GENERALLY HAVE set prices on the Internet in two ways. Many start-ups have offered untenably low prices in a rush to capture first-mover advantage. Many incumbents have simply charged the same prices on-line as they do off-line. Either way, companies are missing a big opportunity.

The fundamental value of the Internet lies not in lowering prices or making them consistent but in optimizing them. After all, if it's easy for customers to compare prices on the Internet, it's also easy for companies to track customers' behavior and adjust prices accordingly.

The Net lets companies optimize prices in three ways. First, it lets them set and announce prices with greater precision. Different prices can be tested easily, and customers' responses can be collected instantly.

Companies can set the most profitable prices, *and* they can tap into previously hidden customer demand.

Second, because it's so easy to change prices on the Internet, companies can adjust prices in response to even small fluctuations in market conditions, customer demand, or competitors' behavior.

Third, companies can use the clickstream data and purchase histories that it collects through the Internet to segment customers quickly. Then it can offer segment-specific prices or promotions immediately.

By taking full advantage of the unique possibilities afforded by the Internet to set prices with precision, adapt to changing circumstances quickly, and segment customers accurately, companies can get their pricing right. It's one of the ultimate drivers of e-business success.

T WO VERY DIFFERENT APPROACHES to pricing— neither optimal—have dominated the sale of goods and services through the Internet. Many start-ups have offered untenably low prices in the rush to capture first-mover advantage. Many incumbents, by contrast, have simply transferred their off-line prices onto the Internet. In some cases, they believe their brand strength inoculates them from the need to price competitively; in other cases, they feel pressure to establish an on-line presence but aren't prepared for the complexities—or potential cannibalization—of multichannel pricing.

Both approaches cause companies to miss a big opportunity. The Internet allows companies to price with far more precision than they can off-line and to create enormous value in the process. Transparency and efficiency, after all, go both ways. Just as it's easy for customers to compare prices on the Internet, so is it easy for companies to track customers' behavior and adjust prices accordingly. But organizations must act quickly and rethink their on-line policies before habit and customer expectations make changes difficult, if not disastrous.

The Reality of E-Pricing

In the absence of hard data, intuition and supposition are still driving many companies' Internet pricing strategies. Some observers insist, for example, that the Internet will be the great equalizer, driving prices down to the lowest level possible, and that customers will take advantage of the Web's transparency by opting exclusively for the lowest prices. In the end, they argue, price will be the most important factor differentiating products and services for on-line consumers, outweighing quality, service, and reputation. And, indeed, when asked, on-line consumers regularly say that far and away the most important factor motivating them to buy on-line is lower prices.

But their behavior tells a different story. A recent study of consumer click-through behavior here at McKinsey & Company has found that most on-line buyers actually shop around very little: 89% of on-line book buyers purchase from the first site they visit; so do 84% of those buying toys, 81% buying music, and 76% buying electronics. Fewer than 10% of Internet users in a separate study of North American consumers turned out to be aggressive bargain hunters. The rest tended to return to the same sites time and again when making on-line purchases.

Nor is price the main consideration for corporate buyers. Businesses buy on-line primarily to lower the total cost of ownership, but price is often a relatively small component of ownership cost. For example, we found that only 30% of B2B purchasing managers identified lower prices as the key benefit to buying on-line. Most said the main advantages come from lowering transaction and search costs—reducing paperwork, for example—and from automating purchasing information to track inventory and make better purchasing decisions. Only 14% of those buyers said they expected to reap lower prices at the expense of suppliers' profit margins. On the contrary, they explicitly recognized that both buyers and suppliers should benefit from reduced transaction costs.

Business-to-business buyers (unlike individual customers) actually do what they say they do in the surveys. Reverse auctions—which are designed to push prices down—are not especially popular, despite all the press they get. Only 15% of the companies that make purchases over the Internet have even tried them. Only 2% of business-to-business buyers prefer reverse auctions to other approaches, and only 3% intend to continue using them in the next year. Interestingly, half of the companies buying through reverse auctions do not choose the low bidder, and 87% of those stay with their current supplier despite the higher price.

Profiting from E-Pricing Flexibility

Of course, even if price is not the most important factor, it does matter; on-line suppliers can't raise prices indiscriminately. Poorly justified price changes can be perceived as capricious—or, worse, deceptive—which can cause long-term damage to a company's price proposition. Ultimately, however, the fundamental value of the Internet lies not in lowering prices but in optimizing them. It gives companies greater precision in setting and announcing prices, more flexibility in changing prices, and better information, which can lead to improved customer segmentation. (See the exhibit "Three Approaches to Improving Pricing.") Let's look at each of these in turn.

PRECISION

All products have a "pricing indifference band," a range of possible prices within which price changes have little or no impact on customers' purchase decisions. These can range as wide as 17 percentage points for branded consumer health-and-beauty products to 10% for engineered industrial components to as narrow as 2% for some financial products. Being at the top rather than the middle or the bottom of this band can have a huge impact on profits. For example, a typical financial services company moving from the middle to the top of a 2% indifference band in setting interest rates for personal loans would increase operating profits by 11% for those products.

Determining the borders of these indifference bands in the physical world is difficult, expensive, and time-consuming. Traditional price-sensitivity research can cost up to $300,000 for each product category and take anywhere from six to ten weeks to complete. It's no wonder that only about 25% of North American companies have conducted such research. Adjusting price changes according to market response keeps companies broadly within their appropriate price range but can't help them pinpoint the precise floor and ceiling.

On the Internet, however, prices can be tested continually in real time, and customers' responses can be instantly received. If, for example, an e-business wants to

Three Approaches to Improving Pricing

Companies can use the Internet to make pricing more precise, to be more adaptable in responding to fluctuations in supply and demand, and to segment customers more effectively.

	Source of value from the Internet	Conditions for selection	B2C examples	B2B examples
Precision	· Greater precision in setting optimal price · Better understanding of zone of price indifference	· Testing needs to be run on at least 200 transactions to be significant	· Toys · Books · CDs	· Maintenance, repair, and operation (MRO) products
Adaptability	· Speed of price change · Ease of response to external shocks to the system (changes in costs or competitive moves, for example)	· Inventory or capacity is perishable · Demand fluctuates over time	· Consumer electronics · Luxury cars	· Chemicals · Raw materials
Segmentation	· Ability to choose creative, accurate segmentation dimensions · Ease in identifying which segment a buyer belongs to · Ability to create barriers between segments	· Different customers value your products' benefits differently · Customer profitability varies widely	· Credit cards · Mortgages · Automobiles	· Industrial components · Business services

determine the sales impact of a 3% price increase, it might test the response by quoting the higher price to every 50th visitor to its site and comparing the purchase rates. These tests can also help a company predict volume fluctuations resulting from price changes that fall outside the indifference band.

This kind of testing can have dramatic results. For example, in an on-line price test conducted by the software-services company Zilliant, an electronics company reduced four products' prices by 7%. Sales volume for three of those products increased by 5% to 20%—not enough to make up for the cost of the price reduction. However, with the fourth product—a high-end model— sales more than doubled. The company analyzed the data and learned that most of that increase came from high schools and universities. The price reduction, it seemed, had uncovered a whole new segment of latent demand. Armed with this knowledge, the company created a special Web site to cater to these buyers and offer them special prices not available to other groups. What's more, the company has also rethought its approach to selling the product to the educational market off-line.

Companies testing prices on-line must take great care not to alienate customers. Recently, Amazon.com angered customers and triggered a wave of bad publicity when in a price test it offered DVD buyers discounts of either 30%, 35%, or 40% off the manufacturer's suggested retail price. When the test was discovered, a vocal portion of those who had been quoted the smaller discount were upset. At every stage, from designing the test through handling responses to complaints or inquiries, companies should remember that the purpose of such testing is to gather information, not revenue. Some companies, when they test a price higher than one previously published, refund the difference as soon as the purchase order is complete by adjusting the invoice or sending a follow-up e-mail.

Companies can also test customers' responses not only to different levels of discounts but also to different approaches to discounting. They can find out if customers respond better to a limited-quantity offer or to a percentage discount, for example. FairMarket, which sets up business-to-business auctions and develops automated-pricing technology, has found that customers buy more quickly and accept higher prices on clearance items when they see a price reduction than when they're told that only a limited quantity is remaining. Testing of this kind is a low-risk way to develop very practical rules of thumb for pricing. Such tests in a bricks-and-mortar store would be extremely expensive and complex, and they wouldn't yield as much in-depth understanding.

ADAPTABILITY

Changing prices in the physical world takes time. Business-to-business markets may need several months to a year to communicate changes to distributors, to print and send out new price lists, and to reprogram their computers. In consumer markets, pricing is a little more flexible, but changes are still costly and time-consuming to carry out. In stores, for example, signs often need to be revised manually every time a price changes. On-line pricing is far more adaptable, allowing companies to make adjustments in a fraction of the time and to profit from even small fluctuations in market conditions, customer demand, and competitors' behavior. Think of the ticketing business, for example. Traditionally, prices on preprinted tickets are set far in advance, and there's no opportunity to recalibrate later.

Tickets.com, by contrast, adjusts concert ticket prices based on supply and demand—and has generated as much as 45% more revenue per event as a result.

Our research suggests that customers don't fight those price adjustments. In fact, Internet sales can often push prices higher, especially when demand fluctuates sharply. Prices for hot products—from video games to luxury cars to concert tickets—are 17% to 45% higher on-line than off because the Web increases the chances of finding a buyer willing to pay a higher price. Taking advantage of this flexibility can improve profits considerably: one consumer electronics company extended the period that a product sold at full price by two weeks, increasing its profits by 17%.

Products in low demand can also command higher prices on-line because of the Internet's ability to expand the buyer base. Aucnet attracts four to five times as many buyers as traditional wholesale car auctions, and FairMarket has been very successful in helping electronics and apparel companies dispose of excess inventory and obsolete products more quickly and profitably.

This pricing flexibility creates an imperative for companies to accurately assess and respond to the overall balance between supply and demand in their industry. For example, when capacity utilization, order lead times, or industrywide inventory levels indicate that products are in great demand across the board, prices might be temporarily raised. Conversely, when overall demand lags, a company might experiment with lower prices, auctions, or targeted short-term promotions. It is estimated that one electronics supplier realized a $25 million profit by adjusting prices faster than other players during a temporary industrywide shortage of key components. The ability to react quickly and decisively is crucial.

SEGMENTATION

It's commonly understood that because different consumers value a product's benefits differently, some are willing to pay more for it than others. But in the off-line world, it's difficult and clumsy to offer different customer segments different prices, particularly in the retail market. A visitor entering a store is usually a statistical mystery. Sales staff have no idea what that customer has bought in the past, what combination of price and benefits would trigger a purchase, whether that person generally buys items at full price or only on sale, or if he needs an incentive to go beyond browsing. The mystery is cleared up on the Internet. On-line companies can segment their customers quickly using many sources of information—everything from clickstream data about the current on-line session to customers' buying histories tracked by cookies created on their own computers.

Once a company has identified an on-line customer segment, it can offer a segment-specific price or promotion immediately. Ford, for example, expects information about its on-line customers to significantly improve the yield from the nearly $10 billion it spends annually on promotional pricing. Efforts like discount financing and cash-back programs have historically been offered to all customers on a broad range of models over a specific period of time. But the Internet will enable Ford to finely target the promotions at just those models that would most benefit and to just those customers who would actually respond.

The Internet also allows companies to identify customers who are happy to pay a premium. For example, an on-line electronic components company uses customers' buying histories to determine if someone is a "core" customer—one that buys a majority of its components from the company—or a "fill-in" customer—one that buys the majority of its components from a competitor and comes to this company only in emergencies, when the competitor does not have the desired component in stock. Through its segmented on-line pricing, this supplier regularly charges fill-in customers as much as 20% more than it charges core customers. And the fill-in customers gladly pay that premium for the assured supply in emergency situations.

Making an On-Line Pricing Strategy Work

How does a company develop and execute an on-line pricing strategy that fully exploits the opportunities afforded by improved pricing precision, adaptability, and segmentation? We've identified three important steps.

IDENTIFY DEGREES OF FREEDOM CONSISTENT WITH STRATEGY AND BRAND

Companies must choose e-pricing approaches that do not inadvertently conflict with key strategic objectives, core business principles, or brand image. For instance, on-line price sensitivity research might suggest that lowering the price for a new product would increase sales profitably, but the price cut wouldn't make sense if a company was trying to position the item as a premium product over the long term. Similarly, a retailer might not be comfortable pursuing a strategy in which widely different prices were offered to different consumers if that was perceived to violate an image of consistency and trustworthiness. But a bank might decide to offer substantially different prices to different customer segments on-line because consumers understand and accept that more profitable, more loyal, more wealthy customers justifiably receive better interest rates on loans.

BUILD APPROPRIATE TECHNOLOGICAL CAPABILITIES

Pursuing the right technology for optimal e-pricing does not necessarily require huge systems investments. Rudimentary tracking and testing initiatives can form a strong foundation for more sophisticated systems, if required later on. Other inexpensive tools include price-tracking software to monitor competitors' prices and on-line surveys to track overall customer price perception.

Ideally, companies should use an array of techniques to inform their pricing strategies by monitoring and responding to the behavior of customers, markets, and competitors. They can:

Test pricing precision, adaptability, and segmentation on-line. Many companies have considered these three modes of e-pricing conservatively because they're locked into an off-line mind-set in which mistakes take a long time to correct. The Internet invites a more dynamic approach in which it's easy to conduct limited tests of alternative prices and pricing structures. These tests can indicate not only at what level to set prices but also which other variables will need to change and how often. A financial services company, for example, may realize tremendous value by changing interest rates hourly, a tactic that would require a highly automated price analysis system. But an industrial manufacturer may find that moving from annual to bimonthly price changes is sufficient. That approach would obviously require less-sophisticated systems to track the peaks and valleys of supply and demand.

Develop early indicators of customer price perception. The Internet grants companies a unique opportunity to get a better handle on customers' price perceptions and pricing indifference bands. One consumer electronics retailer, for example, used a simple on-line survey to help decide how to respond to a proliferation of competitors offering the same products at or below cost. To the managers' surprise, only 5% of respondents cited lower prices as their primary reason for buying from a competitor. That insight led to the decision not to engage in a price war—a move that proved correct. Within months, several pure-play rivals had either gone out of business or announced price increases. Regular surveys can give managers early signals of potential problems or opportunities.

Companies can also track the "book-to-look" ratio as an indicator of customer perception. It's possible to monitor customers' behavior all along the purchasing process, comparing how many people visit a site with how many view and configure a product, check the price, or make a purchase. If the ratio rises above a set threshold, the time may be right for a price increase; alternatively, if it falls, it may be time for a targeted, short-term price promotion.

Identify supply and demand imbalances. To take full advantage of the Internet's flexibility, companies need to spot the shifts in supply and demand that could trigger profitable price changes. Many companies already collect this information for operational purposes, but it's rarely passed along to the pricing group quickly enough to be useful. There is a need for greater coordination to allow pricing and marketing managers to identify these opportunities.

CREATE AN ENTREPRENEURIAL PRICING GROUP

Few pricing organizations are set up to exploit the full potential of e-pricing. This is especially true of incumbent players that have only started to sell on-line; their on-line and off-line pricing strategies usually look exactly the same. Start-up e-businesses often suffer from a related problem for a different reason—they have never developed any sort of pricing capabilities in the first place.

To improve on-line pricing, companies need to replace traditional pricing groups with a new, entrepreneurial pricing organization that is more strategic. (See the exhibit "Old Versus New Pricing Organizations.") It probably should sit at a higher level of the organization than pricing groups generally do, too, so that it has the authority to experiment constantly, to change prices, and to adapt quickly to shifting circumstances. This group will be more analytical, more streamlined, faster, and more flexible. It will be staffed by people who are comfortable with the latest analytical tools and technologies. They will become expert at feeding the information they gather back to the company's off-line channels so that those, too, can become more responsive. We don't know of any pricing organization that does all these things correctly today—but we do know of a few companies that are beginning to move in the right direction.

As PURE INTERNET PLAYS and traditional companies' e-ventures struggle to become profitable, improved
pricing represents a large and as-yet-untapped opportunity. By taking full advantage of the unique possibilities

---

Old Versus New Pricing Organizations

In traditional companies, pricing decisions are made intuitively and globally. But the Internet allows – and requires – companies to price with greater precision, speed, and flexibility.

	From	**To**
Mandate	• To protect business objectives (conservative)	• To aggressively challenge pricing assumptions
Pricing organization	• Decentralized, little authority • Focused on avoiding mistakes	• Centralized, with the authority to lead • Focused on identifying opportunities
Systems and analysis tools	• Largely focused on setting prices in an efficient way • Aggregate pricing data make narrow prescriptions difficult • Pricing decisions based on judgment and experience	• Focused on both setting prices in an efficient way and recommending the most appropriate price • Analysis enables controlled tests of pricing levers • Pricing algorithm and approach explicitly defined – and applied with more rigor
Pricing review processes	• Accountability loosely tied to predictive accuracy	• Predictions continually improved through constant review and discussion of data

afforded by the Internet to set prices with precision, adapt to changing circumstances quickly, and segment customers accurately, companies can get their pricing right. It's one of the ultimate keys to e-business success.

Originally published in February 2001
Reprint R0102J

Making Money with Proactive Pricing

ELLIOT B. ROSS

Executive Summary

ALTHOUGH THE ROOTS of capitalism stretch back many centuries, setting prices remains an inexact science. The pricing decision, one of the most important in business, is also one of the least understood. Many industrial companies, according to this author, habitually set prices reflexively on the basis of simple criteria— to recover costs, to maintain or gain market share, to match competitors. As the author shows, however, some companies have discovered the benefits of thinking more shrewdly about pricing. The rewards of a better understanding of pricing strategy and tactics can be substantial. By carefully studying pertinent information about customers, competitors, and industry economics and by selectively applying appropriate techniques, "proactive pricers" can earn millions of dollars that might otherwise be lost.

SOME OF TODAY'S MOST PROFITABLE industrial companies are by no means the lowest-cost competitors in their industries. By and large, operational efficiency and work force productivity are adequate but not outstanding in these companies. Where these companies really shine is in skillful pricing strategy and tactics. Year in and year out, they manage to outmaneuver their competitors on price. They leave less money on the table in competitive bid situations, they have mastered the art of shaving prices to gain volume without provoking competitive retaliation, and they know when they can quote a higher price without risking the loss of an order or a long-term relationship. By understanding the competitive dynamics of pricing in their industries and the purchasing approaches of their customers, these companies have turned pricing into a potent competitive weapon.

This approach—call it proactive pricing for want of a better label—has in most cases taken shape under the impact of forces that are putting ever-increasing pressures on industrial companies. Across a spectrum of industries ranging from lighting equipment to computer software, customers are gaining power at the expense of suppliers. Competitive intensity is increasing, causing specialty products to evolve into near-commodities. Computerized information systems enable the purchaser to compare price and performance factors with unprecedented ease and accuracy. Improved communications and increased use of telemarketing and computer-aided selling have opened up many markets to additional competitors. In this environment, the penalties for maladroit pricing practices are fast becoming prohibitive.

Take the case of a Midwestern electromechanical components manufacturer, which recently found itself in a tough spot. With market share stagnant and industry prices edging downward, the company's margins were taking a terrible beating, and there was no relief in sight. In an effort to gain share and restore income levels, the marketing vice president ordered prices to be cut by an average of 7%. Within three weeks, however, the move had provoked severe price cuts from the company's major competitors and set off a full-scale price war. Prices swiftly declined in a kind of death spiral that soon had everyone in the industry doing business at a loss.

What the initiator of this downward spiral had failed to realize was that conditions in the industry—a high-fixed-cost, high-contribution-margin business—were ripe for a price war: there was substantial excess capacity at the time, and the major competitors were desperate to hold their own share positions. Ironically, the unfortunate executive who had started it all by failing to anticipate his competitors' reaction to his ill-fated initiative, saw his company as the victim of an unprovoked attack. This misapprehension was natural enough: all the information the company had about current price levels in the industry was what it had gleaned from the bids on orders lost to competitors. Where pricing was concerned, the company had weighed its options with all the weights on one side of the scale.

Because the consequences of a rash pricing initiative can be so disastrous, most managers are disposed to play it safe and price defensively, keeping a close eye on their competitors and parrying as best they can any pricing moves that could cost them orders or threaten their position with marginal accounts. By adopting a reactive pricing posture, they escape the pitfalls of reckless price leadership. But over time they may also pay a heavy penalty in forgone profits—money left on the table on hundreds or even thousands of orders.

Today's more sophisticated industrial marketers realize that they need not put up with either the risks of rash price pioneering or the invisible costs associated with a reactive pricing posture. Some increasingly popular proactive pricing techniques enable aggressive companies to reap the rewards of intelligent pricing initiatives while minimizing the risks of competitive retaliation.

To see how they attain this objective, let us explore some frequently overlooked aspects of pricing in the industrial environment. We shall then look at the major elements of pricing strategy and tactics as practiced by these companies and conclude with some observations on building a system for effective pricing.

The Dynamics of Pricing

The secret of improving pricing performance without the risk of damaging market repercussions lies in understanding how pricing works in an industry and particularly how customers perceive prices (see *Exhibit 1* for a simple diagnostic test of pricing policies). In general, in comparing suppliers' offerings, a customer will measure purchase prices against the relative value of the performance it expects from each product and the service it expects from the product's supplier. Of the three factors—performance, service, price—price seems to be the least subjective. What could be less ambiguous than a number?

As the customer perceives it, however, price is in fact a relatively subjective thing. The dollars-and-cents price level is only one element in perceived price. Equally

Exhibit 1.   Are you a proactive pricer?

The 20 questions below provide a simple diagnostic test of your pricing strategy and tactics. If you can answer no to the first 10 and yes to the second 10, you are a shrewd pricer. If the results are otherwise, it may be rewarding to reconsider how you set prices.

1. Is your market share constant or declining while prices are falling in real terms?
2. Do you have a nagging suspicion—but no real evidence—that you are regularly bidding too high for contracts?
3. Do your salespeople keep complaining that your prices are several percentage points too high although your share is holding steady?
4. Do your contribution margins for the same product vary widely from customer to customer?
5. Are you unsure who is the industry price leader?
6. Do your pricing approval levels seem to be functioning more as a volume discount device than as a control mechanism?
7. Would you have trouble describing your competitors' pricing strategies?
8. Do you find that too many pricing decisions seem aimed at gaining volume, despite an overall nonvolume strategy?
9. Are most of your prices set at minimum approval levels?
10. Do your competitors seem to anticipate your pricing actions with ease, while theirs often take you by surprise?

11. Do you have a planned method of communicating price changes to customers and distributors?
12. Do you know how long to wait before following a competitor's price change?
13. Are your prices set to reflect such customer-specific costs as transportation, set-up charges, design costs, warranty, sales commissions, and inventory?
14. Do you know how long it takes each of your major competitors to follow one of your price moves?
15. Do you know the economic value of your product to your customers?
16. Do you use the industry's price/volume curve as an analytic aid to price setting?
17. Do you know whether you would be better off making a single large price change or several small changes?
18. Do you know how to go about establishing price leadership in your industry?
19. Are your prices based strictly on your own costs?
20. Do you have a consistent and effective policy for intracompany pricing?

important, in many cases, is the way the price is structured. For example, some industrial companies quote
set-up costs as a separate charge to maintain the appearance of low unit prices. Volume discounts, year-end
rebates, credit terms, and inclusion of transportation
costs are other methods of structuring and communicating prices to influence the customer's perception.

The timing of price changes is another factor influencing the customer's perception. For example, customers may perceive a company that follows its competitor's price increase announcements by two or three
weeks as a low-price supplier, even though the price
changes both companies announce may take effect on
the same day.

Inadequate information compounds the difficulty of
making the right decisions on price level, structure, and
timing. Lacking precise internal cost data, a clear
market-price reference point, or the value customers
place on the product, manufacturers have to rely on
guesswork in setting price level; and if they don't understand the thinking that goes into customers' purchase
decisions, they are likely to structure and communicate
prices in a counterproductive way. Finally, uncertainty
about such things as future rates of inflation, changes in
costs, competitors' actions, and customers' reactions
complicates the correct timing of price changes.

In the perfect markets that theoretical economists
envision, of course, pricing freedom doesn't exist: the
point where the demand curve intersects the supply
curve reflects the collective costs and capacities of all
suppliers and determines the price. However, successful
industrial marketers have understood and exploited the
fact that a multitude of imperfections in the marketplace
affect the dynamics of supply and demand in the real

world of industrial products. These imperfections determine the degree of pricing freedom and open the door to significant profit improvement through proactive pricing.

THE PRICE BAND

When a large number of individual orders for a particular industrial product in a particular market are plotted on a graph against price, something close to a normal frequency distribution curve is likely to emerge. Because of differences in prevailing practices with respect to list prices, automatic discount points, and so on, the shape of the curve varies from industry to industry, but a spread of ten percentage points on either side of an average industry price level is not uncommon (see *Exhibit 2*).

Exhibit 2. *Typical Distribution of Orders for a Product*

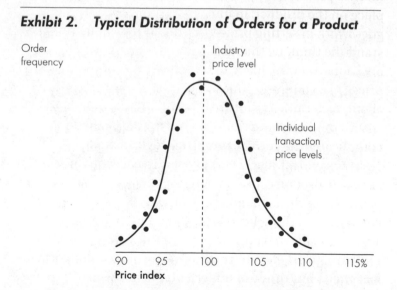

Regardless of its shape, the existence of this price band in virtually every industrial market results from variations or imperfections in both demand and supply factors. On the demand side, customer inertia—the tendency to stick with an established supplier—often contributes greatly to the spread of prices. In some industries, getting a new customer's business is rarely possible without a substantial price inducement. Sometimes inducements are needed because the customer is averse to the business and personal risks involved in changing to a new supplier whose quality and reliability are untested; sometimes inducements are a matter of straight economics. (One supplier of plastic resins, for example, reports that a 3% to a 5% price break is usually needed to persuade a typical customer to change suppliers, simply because it would cost the customer about $75,000 to clean out its system and put in a new product.) And even within an industry, customers differ in their buying practices, in the importance they attach to price, in their willingness to pay extra for product quality, performance, or delivery, and in their responsiveness to terms and discounts.

Price visibility is another factor that influences the width of the price band: in commodity-type industries, where every customer knows what its competitors are paying for the same product, there is little if any price variation. In contrast, in industries where price visibility is low, the price band is usually wide. Finally, customer purchasing power is often reflected in the width of the price band. A massive purchaser like Ford or Procter & Gamble tends to limit the supplier's freedom to raise prices, while fragmentation of market power among a host of small customers tends to enhance it.

On the supply side, differences among competitors—such as in run lengths and transportation costs; in product quality, features, and performance; in service; in pricing terms and conditions; or in sales efficiency and effectiveness—contribute to price variations. The level of competitive intensity in an industry further affects price variation and hence the degree of freedom available to the proactive pricer; the higher the ratio of customers to suppliers, the wider the price band.

The ice-cream industry provides a simple illustration of how the price band can vary between market segments (see *Exhibit 3*). In the case of the generic product, the equivalent of a commodity, the consumer price band is very narrow—plus or minus 2 cents a serving. But in

Exhibit 3.   The Price Band in Ice Cream

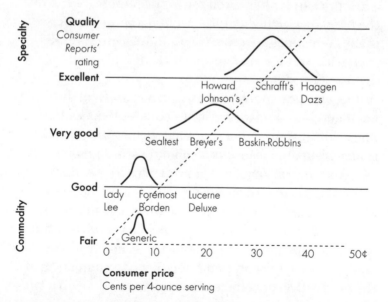

Consumer price
Cents per 4-ounce serving

the specialty segments the price band broadens to plus
or minus 10 cents per serving. This range of prices
depends partly on the way customers perceive the relative value of different brands of ice cream that are sold in
that segment and partly on the competitive intensity in
each segment.

PRICING STRATEGY & TACTICS

In light of the complex ways in which each variable influences a company's latitude for action, some of the most
adroit industrial pricing practitioners are careful to distinguish between pricing strategy and pricing tactics.
Moves aimed at shifting the company's position within
the existing price band of the industry are seen as pricing
tactics. A supplier normally takes its market share from a
portion of the price band: it may opt for high volume at
a low price or for lower volume at the high-price end of
the band to earn higher total profit dollars. (In practice,
many companies are more preoccupied with volume
than with profit share and give little thought to this
degree of freedom.)

Pricing strategy, in contrast, aims at shifting the price
band and the company's relative competitive position.
Such shifting may entail changing the product, the customer group, the distribution channels, or the sales strategy—all with the objective of bringing about a movement of the industry price level.

The degree of strategic pricing freedom open to any
supplier depends on both the product's perceived value
to the customer and the competitive intensity of the
business, as defined in terms of either the uniqueness of
the product or the number of suppliers bidding on a typi-

cal order. At one extreme of the competitive intensity scale is the specialty manufacturer of a patented product with unique performance characteristics. This sole supplier has tremendous latitude with respect to price; it can virtually set a price at any level it wishes and in effect choose a position on the demand curve. At the other end of the spectrum, where several suppliers are fighting for every order and where the laws of supply and demand dictate prices, management has no real strategic pricing freedom. At best, a company can try to anticipate how specific changes in capacity and cost position on its own part or that of its competitors will affect the price level.

The second determinant of a supplier's strategic pricing freedom, the product's perceived value to the customer, can be defined as the benefits the customer expects to achieve from its purchase relative to an alternative product or to no purchase at all. At one end of the scale stands the product that uniquely fills a vital need, such as the CAT scanner. (In these cases the value is sufficiently high to allow the supplier to raise prices.) At the other end are products that can be differentiated from substitutes only on the basis of net price, such as the corn syrup sold to soft drink manufacturers when it is cheaper than cane sugar. In between lie the industrial products in which the supplier has room to cut its production costs—though not, as a rule, to raise its prices.

THE PRICING FRAMEWORK

In combination, these two variables—competitive intensity and perceived value—provide a useful framework for thinking about pricing (see *Exhibit 4*). Any business can be assigned to one of four categories within this

Exhibit 4. Price Bands in the Pricing Framework

		Perceived economic value	**High**		

Examples

Drugs

Water-treatment chemical

Wire-line services

Specialty

Pricing is a high-leverage independent variable. Price band is wide and easily moved.

Engineered commodity

Pricing is a semi-independent variable. Price band is of varying widths and difficult to move.

Examples

Personal computers

Copy machines

Steam turbines

Jet engines

35 mm cameras

CRTs

Examples

Xenography, 1955

Polavision, 1975

Genetic engineering 1984

Threshold product

Pricing is an independent variable. Price band is wide but hard to move.

Commodity

Pricing is a dependent variable based on supply and demand. Price band is narrow and very hard to move.

Examples

Aluminum

PVC

Steel

Caustic soda

Fasteners

Low   High

Competitive intensity

framework. In the upper left-hand quadrant are specialty products such as prescription drugs, wire-line services in the oil field, and water-treatment chemicals—businesses characterized by high perceived value and low competitive intensity. Pricing is a high-leverage independent variable in such businesses. In the lower right-hand quadrant are products like steel, PVC, caustic soda, aluminum, and standard fasteners—commodity businesses characterized by low economic value and high competitive intensity. Here, pricing is a dependent variable based on the intersection of supply and demand curves. In the lower left-hand quadrant are businesses like xerography back in 1955, Polavision in 1975, and genetic engineering in 1984—unique products whose economic value to the customer is unknown. In these businesses, competitive intensity is very low, and pricing, though subject to certain constraints, can be considered a largely independent variable. Finally, in the upper right-hand quadrant are engineered commodities like cathode-ray tubes, jet engines, steam turbines, personal computers, and copying machines, characterized by both high economic value and high competitive intensity. For these manufacturers, pricing is a semi-independent variable, limited mainly by the competitive intensity factor.

The available latitude for proactive pricing in an industrial market can easily be seen when the pricing framework is coupled with the concept of the price band. In the specialty quadrant, the price band is usually both wide and easy to shift. Customarily, a threshold product has a wide band that is difficult to move until the market begins to recognize the value of the product. In the engineered commodity segment, the band may vary in width but is almost always immovable. In the commodity segment, the band is both narrow and fixed.

Proactive Pricing Strategy

Marketers who understand where their products or businesses fit in the pricing framework can easily take advantage of pricing opportunities. In seeking to capitalize on these opportunities, they tend to focus on four questions: (1) Is the price accurately keyed to the value to the customer? (2) Will the price help the purchasing decision makers look good? (3) How will prices change over time? (4) How will competitors respond?

PRICING TO REFLECT PERCEIVED VALUE

On the principle that effective product pricing must be based on customer economics, successful industrial marketers, when calculating how much financial incentive their prices should reflect, give careful consideration to the cost and the risk the customer may incur in purchasing their products.

Consider the example of a numerically controlled machine tool that not only offers the customer lower start-up and operating costs but works to closer tolerances than the best available alternative. Altogether, these benefits may be worth an extra $30,000 to the customer. But the customer may face certain risks as well: the union may object, the maintenance staff may not be qualified to service the new device, and/or customers may not want to pay much extra for better finish. Extensive discussions with customers may lead the supplier to conclude that these costs and risks probably reduce the $30,000 benefit by $12,000 and that a further $2,500 will be needed to induce customers to switch. The manufacturer would then set the price premium for its new product at $15,500 ($30,000 − [$12,000 + $2,500]).

Some successful marketers routinely apply this kind of analysis before they make any major commitment to a new industrial product. After having used the results to assess the likely returns from the new product and the switching cost (and hence the amount of the required customer inducement) likely to be involved, these marketers find that they can decide much more confidently whether to proceed with a major resource commitment.

TARGETING THE PURCHASING DECISION MAKER

In approaching any important decision, proactive pricers take care to ensure that the price is sensitive to the requirements of the individuals in the customer's organization who will influence the buying decision. It is important to give the buyer a price that will help him or her to look good. In many cases, this task is anything but a simple matter, because it must take into account the distinctive buying processes that, with innumerable individual variations, characterize customers in a particular industry.

Consider the case of the specialty chemical industry. Here the purchasing decision is the culmination of three distinct stages: (1) product testing and demonstration, (2) product specification, and (3) ongoing purchase. At the first stage, the typical decision maker is an R&D manager; at the second, R&D shares responsibility with other management; at the final stage, the purchasing department makes the ongoing buying decisions subject to the approval of top management. At each stage, price is a factor in the decision, and an understanding of the needs and motivations of the decision makers along the way is basic to successful pricing.

When a new product is under consideration, the supplier needs to demonstrate to the decision maker—usually an R&D scientist with a tight budget and an outsize workload—that the product promises the company some benefit. If this benefit is substantial enough in relation to the price, the decision maker will be inclined to pass the product ahead to the specification stage. Here price tends to become a central issue. Besides providing a clear inducement to buy, the price must be thoughtfully structured and communicated. For example, managers who are judged on their contributions to longer-term profitability may benefit from life-cycle pricing, which takes into account the various costs of a component over its useful life.

Success in securing repeat orders often depends on the timing of price increases. Many purchasing people, for example, are evaluated on the basis of material variance against standard costs that increase annually to account for expected inflation. Accordingly, they routinely compare product cost increases with several different inflation indices. A supplier who attempts to raise prices ahead of inflation can expect to be passed over. Proactive pricers who try to hold their increase below the inflation rate can make the purchasing manager look like a hero. Often, by doing so, proactive suppliers succeed in cementing a sole-source position.

Skillful use of discounts, payment terms, financing, spare-parts prices, consigned stock, warranties, and other techniques affords these suppliers the flexibility to communicate price in a way that is sensitive to the needs of the customer decision makers. Consider, for example, a situation in which an initial equipment purchase locks in a number of subsequent expenditures (e.g., for spare parts) and the purchasing manager is evaluated on initial expenditures. Here, shrewd suppliers price the original equipment relatively low and the spare parts relatively high. This is a common practice in aerospace components, where the original supplier is virtually guaranteed a 20-year stream of spare-parts orders. (This tactic can, however, be overdone, as some Defense Department suppliers have discovered.) Again, where the performance of the purchasing decision maker is assessed on the basis of unit costs rather than on his or her contributions to long-term profitability, it makes better sense to structure the price as a low piece rate plus an initial set-up charge than to prorate the set-up charge as part of the piece rate.

Beyond securing the initial sale, some suppliers use discounts to induce sales in large quantities or at times that optimize their manufacturing or distribution costs. In process industries, seasonal discounts help to smooth out the demand patterns. One bulk chemicals supplier offers a 3% discount during the first ten days of each quarter, solely to counter the sales representatives' tendency to relax at the beginning of a bonus period. Other manufacturers are beginning to experiment with similar approaches.

CHANGING THE PRICE

The issues of when, how often, and how much to change prices are complicated by inflation, which drives costs up, and the experience curve, which—especially in the case of new products—tends to bring them down. In some industries, as a manufacturer doubles its cumulative volume, it can expect its costs to go down by 20% to 30% because of improved direct labor productivity, scale economies, technological improvements, and the like. Sophisticated marketers take inflation and the experience curve carefully into account as they approach the risky initial pricing decision for a new product or prepare to enter a new customer segment. Over time, cost changes and competitive actions will create a need for price changes. Starting too low makes it hard to raise prices to achieve an acceptable return, while starting (and staying) too high may frustrate the company's efforts to achieve the volume necessary for the new product's survival. Or if, despite unduly high prices, attractive volume should develop, competitors will inevitably be attracted into the market and prices will go down.

Inflation obliges every supplier to monitor its costs so as to ensure continuing profitability. Fortunately, cost reductions resulting from the experience-curve phenomenon may partly or wholly offset the impact of inflation. An understanding of this process—which, again, is an industry-specific phenomenon—enables proactive pricers to forecast with reasonable accuracy when and by how much they must adjust prices to maintain their margins.

Proactive pricers realize, however, that the timing of change in price level or structure and the way they communicate such change strongly affect how new customers and competitors see them. These pricers know too that customers, especially those for whom the product represents a major item of cost, value the consistency and predictability of price changes. Leadership in raising prices can help build attractive margins but may be costly in terms of customer perception since the first to announce an increase is often seen as the high-price supplier. Proactive pricers, however, often take the lead in introducing new pricing structures or communications methods as a means of gaining competitive differentiation.

Proactive suppliers usually time price changes to the anticipated reactions of customers and competitors rather than to the results of their own analysis of costs. They know that accounting-driven cost and price changes are normally predictable and that both competitors and customers can exploit these changes to the supplier's disadvantage.

CALCULATING COMPETITORS' RESPONSES

The need for an industrial marketer to consider its competitors' probable responses in planning its own price moves is obvious. In relatively stable commodity or near-commodity industries, the price behavior of established competitors tends to be predictable, so that the price leader seldom has to worry about what to expect. Nearer the specialty-product end of the industrial spectrum, however, the exercise of prediction becomes both more complex, because perceived product value is a function of having many variables, and more speculative, because competitive behavior is more volatile.

Still, sophisticated industrial marketers in these industries succeed surprisingly well in anticipating the reactions of their principal competitors to major price moves. In most cases the secret seems to be nothing more mysterious than patient gathering, collation, and analysis of bits and pieces of information about key competitors—their costs, the details of their business systems, their approaches to technology, product design, marketing and distribution, and any other key functions. Some notably successful proactive pricers have their most knowledgeable managers act out the roles of key competitors to help predict likely reactions to a proposed price initiative or probable bids on a major order. The pricing question that should be asked in such cases is not "What price will it take to win this order?" but "Do we want this order, given the price our competitors are likely to quote?"

Legitimate sources of competitive intelligence range from advertising and product literature to trade gossip picked up by salespeople. Companies that have tried thoroughly debriefing their sales forces about particular competitors have often been astonished at the sheer volume of information that collectively surfaces and at the usefulness of the insights that can emerge once this information is fitted together.

Because an understanding of each competitor's pricing process can provide important clues to its responses, some sophisticated marketers routinely instruct their salespeople to note and report the prices quoted by specific competitors in various marketing situations, with the aim of assembling a statistically valid sample. Supplemented by insights into competitors' organizations, the caliber of their people, and the share and margin pressures they face, the resulting statistical picture enables these marketers to predict with reasonable confidence whether a given price move will secure the intended competitive advantage.

From Strategy to Tactics

The value of the tools and concepts that today's proactive pricers use is not confined to major decisions on the level, structuring, and timing of product prices. Day-by-day attention to the pricing of individual orders, based on the same principles, has enabled many companies to improve their positions in the industry price band (and hence, over the long run, their profitability) without provoking serious competitive reactions.

SETTING THE PRICE LEVEL

A marketing manager can evaluate the profit opportunities inherent in day-to-day tactical pricing by looking at the money left on the table for orders the company has won. One U.S. industrial manufacturer decided to spot-check five out of several dozen orders for an engineered commodity that his salespeople had won over a one-month period. He discovered that his winning prices had averaged fully 5% below those of the next lowest bidder.

Because salespeople are normally eager to report competitors' prices on the orders that they have lost but not on those they have won, unwary executives can easily get the impression that competitors always have the lowest prices in the industry and may pass up the opportunity to put through price increases that could stick.

Proactive pricers are not so credulous. They provide each price decision maker with explicit guidelines that indicate whether—because of the company's cost position and the customer's circumstances and characteristics—the price quoted on a given order should be equal to, lower than, or higher than the competition's. As illustrated in *Exhibit 5,* the guidelines one well-managed industrial company uses can be keyed to two customer-specific factors: the price sensitivity and the price transparency (how well-informed competitors are likely to be about the price quoted on a given order). When the customer's price sensitivity is high, it makes good sense to match or underprice competitors; the reverse is true if it is low. For a highly "transparent" customer—one who will show every competitor every other competitor's price—it usually is best, even at the risk of losing some orders, to price high, encouraging competitors to think that the industry price level is higher than it actually is. With a relatively "opaque" customer, on the other hand, this manufacturer tends to price low—particularly where the cost to serve the account in question is low—as a means of safely gaining volume without provoking the competition to respond in kind.

Exhibit 5. *Guidelines for Tactical Pricing*

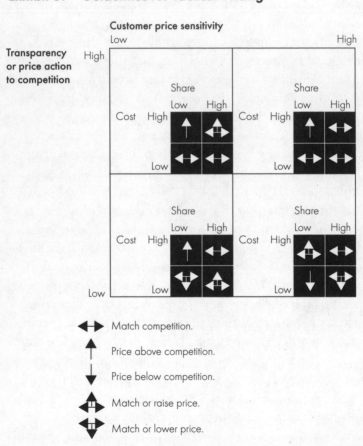

Timing Price Changes

Nimble, but by no means hasty, response to competitors' price moves is a hallmark of today's best-managed industrial marketing organizations. These companies are thoughtful price tacticians as well as skilled strategists. How quickly should the company follow a competitor's price cut? How long, if at all, should the company put off following a price increase? One business has based its guidelines on two key variables: (1) its share strength in the market segment involved and (2) its cost relative to that of the competition (see *Exhibit 6*).

Some sophisticated marketers who consistently practice price-following have mastered the art of building customer loyalty and even attracting new business by playing the role of the low-cost supplier who never initiates a price increase and follows competitors' increases only reluctantly. Success in this role owes much to careful calculation of the time interval between competitive price move and corporate response. Too short a lag, and the policy may not register with customers; too long, and money will be left on the table. In one case in which customer interviews indicated that a six-week time lag following a competitor's price increase would suffice to reinforce the low-cost supplier image, the company discovered that it was actually lagging behind competitors by two to eight months because of its own internal delays in changing prices. A clear-cut timing plan for putting price changes into effect and streamlining the decision process corrected this problem.

Successful proponents of proactive pricing often outmaneuver their competitors by cleverly adapting the price structure to the customer's purchasing procedures and criteria. The approach that a big manufacturer of power distribution equipment follows illustrates the point. His electrical utility customers buy on an annual basis, asking for bids once a year and subsequently ordering monthly installments of the total order placed at the beginning of the year. Suppliers to this industry structure their prices in different ways: some quote fixed prices for the full year; others give firm prices for the first two quarters, with monthly escalation thereafter; still others quote firm prices for one quarter, again with monthly escalation thereafter; and a fourth group includes an escalation clause taking effect from the end of the first month.

Exhibit 6. *How to Time Pricing Moves*

		Cost relative to competition in the segment	
		Lower	Higher
Share position in the segment	Strong	Meet price drops quickly–3 weeks.	Meet price drops quickly to protect share–1 week. Follow price increases quickly–1 week.
	Weak	Follow price increases grudgingly–3 months.	Meet price drops grudgingly–2 months. Follow price increases quickly–1 week.

The supplier in question took the trouble to find out how all the customers in its market evaluated suppliers' bids. Fully a third of the customers, it discovered, ranked bids on the basis of year-end prices alone, while one in four examined prices in January without regard to escalation clauses. The manufacturer, whose policy had been to price for a single quarter with monthly escalation thereafter, switched to quoting a fixed inclusive price to the first group of customers, and monthly escalation over the whole year to the second group. The effect on its winning-bids ratio and its margins was dramatic. Now competitors have belatedly begun to follow suit.

A Pricing System for Profits

Proactive pricing approaches are more likely to succeed if they are supported by sound pricing systems. Such systems are not always easy to develop, and their effective implementation takes time and perseverance. The elements of a successful pricing system include the following:

- First, marketers must gather a great deal of information about market and customer characteristics, competitor capabilities and actions, and internal capabilities and costs. After thorough and imaginative analysis, marketers can use this information to draw up pricing policies and guidelines that can then be translated into customer-specific pricing tactics.

- Second, collection and analysis of price data for each product must begin early in the development process and continue throughout the product's life. Sources of customer and competitor data are the sales force,

targeted customer interviews, competitor sales literature, trade publications, security analysts' reports,
and former employees of customers and competitors.
Proactive pricers use information gathered from these
sources—data on competitors' product performance,
cost structure, current and expected capacities, and
pricing strategies as well as on customer product
expectations and buying processes—to stay a jump
ahead of the rest of their industry in pricing skill and
sophistication. Good market, competitive, and internal data give top management a vital edge in developing pricing strategy and put a potent competitive
weapon in the hands of the middle managers and
salespeople who will be making the day-to-day pricing
decisions.

• Third, successful companies are structured to take
advantage of the data needed to support effective
pricing. Because this data must be up-to-the-minute
and must be drawn from a wide variety of sources,
organizing to collect and use it is always something
of a challenge. Responsibility for this effort is normally lodged in the marketing function, usually not
with marketing research staffers but with product or
market managers so as to capitalize on their close-
ness to the customers and daily involvement with
competition.

• Fourth, flexible and responsive systems for collecting
and using pricing data are characteristic of the most
successful pricing practitioners. Many companies
have developed special incentives to encourage salespeople to bring in good customer and competitive
data, especially prices on both won and lost orders.

Most also provide their pricing decision makers with on-line linkages to the product cost systems and with quick access to current customer-specific costs. One company I know reports a very high payoff from an approval and tracking system that links each pricing decision to an individual and provides those concerned (and their immediate superiors) with feedback on their performance, in terms of their "win" rates and actual profitability.

- Fifth, successful pricers usually assign more and better people than their competitors to jobs involving collecting, analyzing, and using price information. Aware that poor pricing performance is often more a reflection of overworked and underqualified staff than of ineffective pricing strategies or tactics, proactive companies fill these positions with people who combine quantitative skills with a sense for competitive dynamics.

- Finally, effective control and feedback on results are essential to the success of a proactive pricing system. Management must have a reliable way of tracking and evaluating the pricing decisions made by each individual with pricing responsibilities in the organization—so that it will know, among other things, if consistently specified approval levels are being observed in day-to-day practice.

The value of a superior pricing information system can often be measured in hard cash. One company, determined to improve its pricing information, started by revising its accounting data to reflect fixed and variable costs accurately by product and by market. By surveying the sales force, it created a pricing history by customer and product type of each key competitor as well as a profile of the buying process of each major customer. Finally, it provided each pricing decision maker with a personal microcomputer, access to three data bases (cost, competitor, and customer), guidelines on pricing strategy, and feedback on individual performance. In less than a year (and at a time of declining market demand), its margins improved by several percentage points, representing almost $25 million in added profits.

In most industrial companies major pricing opportunities are waiting to be realized. They exist for a number of reasons. For one, most managers are unaware of the latitude that the price band affords and hence of the opportunity costs of passive, purely reactive pricing policies. For another, not many companies really understand their customers' economics and buying behavior. Taking advantage of proactive pricing opportunities, if done intelligently, entails little risk. Improvements in pricing, moreover, are possible in many situations without provoking competitive retaliation, and they are often sustainable because the competitors cannot readily detect them.

A final attraction of proactive pricing is that the approach itself carries such a low price tag. Installing a proactive pricing system entails limited investment, minimal added expense, and minor organizational adjustments. But the payoff is usually both substantial and quick in coming. Given a solid understanding of the dynamics of price level, structure, and timing; knowledge of the customer; an up-to-date data base; and consistency in execution, any industrial company can successfully use pricing proactively as a tool for building and sustaining profits.

Pricing Dilemmas in an Earlier Age

THE DIVERGENCE BETWEEN the merchants and most of the rest of the Puritan population manifested itself more explicitly in public condemnations for malpractices in trade, particularly overcharging, usury, taking advantage of a neighbor's need. The public clamor that accompanied one such incident grew to such proportions as to indicate that an important source of discontent had been touched.

Robert Keayne was a typical self-made tradesman of London. Starting as a butcher's son in Windsor he had risen through apprenticeship in London to prominence as a merchant tailor. Transplanted to New England in 1635, he was received into the church, made a freeman of the corporation, and immediately assumed a leading position in local affairs. He moved into a house and shop on the southwest corner of Cornhill and King streets in the heart of Boston, one lot distant from the First Church and facing the central market square. Drawing on the "two or 3000 lb [£] in good estate" he had brought with him, he reestablished contact with his London friends and commenced his career as a retailer of imported manufactures. For four years he rode the wave of the inflation, selling badly needed goods to the immigrants for whatever prices he could get. But in November 1639 he was struck down by both church and state. Keayne was charged in General Court with "taking above six-pence in the shilling profit; in some above eight-pence; and in some small things, above two for one."

It had all started with a bag of nails he had sold at what he claimed was a perfectly reasonable price.

Once this single charge had exposed the merchant to public censure, a variety of other accusations, such as overcharging for "great gold buttons," a bridle, and a skein of thread, were fired at him. Haled before the highest court he was made to face a barrage of denunciation.

So far only the civil sword had struck. The church then took up the matter. The elders studied "how farr I was guilty of all those claymors and rumors that then I lay under," and exposed his defense to a most "exquisite search." Though he escaped excommunication, a fact he later boasted of, he was given a severe admonition ". . . in the Name of the Church for selling his wares at excessive Rates, to the Dishonor of Gods name, the Offence of the Generall Cort, and the Publique scandall of the Cuntry." It took a "penetentiall acknowledgment" of his sin to regain full membership in the church.

Reprinted by permission of the publishers from The New England Merchants in the Seventeenth Century by Bernard Bailyn, Cambridge, Mass: Harvard University Press, Copyright © 1955 by the President and Fellows of Harvard College.

Originally published in November–December 1984
Reprint 84614

About the Contributors

WALTER BAKER is an associate at McKinsey & Company, Inc., in Atlanta.

MARK E. BERGEN holds the Carolyn I. Anderson Professorship in Business Education Excellence and Marketing/Logistics Management at the University of Minnesota's Carlson School of Management in Minneapolis.

SCOTT DAVIS is principal and founder of Strategic Marketing Decisions, a consultancy in Sacramento, California.

JOEL DEAN was president of Joel Dean Associates and professor of business economics at Columbia University. Mr. Dean was formerly on the faculty of the University of Chicago. During World War II, he was head of machinery price control and later of fuel rationing.

ROBERT J. DOLAN is Dean and the Stephen M. Ross Professor of Business at the University of Michigan's Ross School of Business. He was formerly the Edward W. Carter Professor of Business Administration at Harvard Business School.

JOHN GOURVILLE is a professor at Harvard Business School in Boston.

MICHAEL V. MARN is pricing consultant in the Cleveland, Ohio, office of McKinsey & Company, Inc.

AKSHAY R. RAO is the General Mills Professor of Marketing and Co-Director of the Institute for Research in Marketing at the University of Minnesota's Carlson School of Management in Minneapolis.

ROBERT L. ROSIELLO in principal in McKinsey & Company's New York City office.

ELLIOT B. ROSS is cofounder of The MFL Group, an executive consulting and coaching firm, and was previously head of McKinsey's worldwide marketing practice.

MANMOHAN S. SODHI is a professor at the City University's Cass Business School in London.

NAVDEEP S. SODHI is a pricing strategist who has worked in the airline, medical device, and manufacturing industries. He was recently director of global pricing at Kennametal Inc., a tooling solutions company based in Latrobe, Pennsylvania.

DILIP SOMAN is a professor of marketing at the University of Toronto's Rotman School of Management.

CRAIG ZAWADA is an associate principal at McKinsey & Company in Pittsburgh, Pennsylvania.

Index